1982

P. T. FORSYTH AND
THE CURE OF SOULS

P. T. FORSYTH
and the Cure of Souls

An Appraisement
and Anthology of his practical writings

BY HARRY ESCOTT

London

GEORGE ALLEN & UNWIN LTD

RUSKIN HOUSE   MUSEUM STREET

First published in 1948
by Epworth Press as
PETER TAYLOR FORSYTH:
DIRECTOR OF SOULS

THIS REVISED AND ENLARGED EDITION
PUBLISHED 1970
by George Allen & Unwin Ltd

© *George Allen & Unwin Ltd., 1970*

ISBN:0 04248008 6

PRINTED IN GREAT BRITAIN
BY BARNICOTTS LTD
TAUNTON, SOMERSET

To

THE GROWING BAND OF DISCIPLES
WHO HAVE FOUND IN P. T. FORSYTH
INSPIRATION FOR PRAYER
ACTION AND THOUGHT

If social duty be unreal, all is unreal. Our real and great hope is not that one day we shall die to the world, but that this day we live to others and to God.

—*P.T.F.*

Acknowledgements

THE author wishes to thank Mrs Jessie Forsyth Andrews for generous permission to quote from her father's books, sermons, and pamphlets, and for help and encouragement given to him in the production of the anthology; Mr J. W. K. Tarling, of the Independent Press, for allowing him to take extracts from *This Life and the Next*, *The Work of Christ*, and *Positive Preaching and the Modern Mind*, and other books of Dr Forsyth's; the Rev. F. W. Bell, for his help and wise suggestions, and all others who by their kindness have made the production of this volume possible. His thanks are due to Dr Frank Cumbers of the Epworth Press for his kindness and co-operation. He would also express indebtedness to the Rev. Stanley I. Blomfield, an old student of Dr Forsyth's, for affording access to notes of a hitherto unpublished series of the doctor's addresses to his students. This book would have been impoverished but for Mr Blomfield's generosity. He would also like to add the name of the Rev. W. F. Rowlands, BA, BD, who corrected the original book in manuscript, wrote the Preface, and whose fellowship in things Forsythian made the writing of the volume a rewarding experience.

H.E.

GLASGOW
April, 1966

Contents

Anthology Part Three: The Perfection of Faith

Anthology Part Four: The Soul of Prayer

xi

THIS study of Dr Forsyth as a spiritual guide was published in 1948 by the Epworth Press, with the title *Peter Taylor Forsyth: Director of Souls*. The book was a lowly yet a pioneer volume in a line of books about the theologian that have appeared in the last two decades.

It stood alone as a vade-mecum of the doctor's devotional direction, and in that humble place it probably still stands, for all its faults.

In its original format it has proved useful, we are happy to know, to ministers and laymen alike, to the learned and the simple; and, in this sense, at least, the book would have delighted the heart of its great exemplar. But, unavoidably, the years have revealed some errors of fact, as well as infelicities of expression, in the *Appraisement*, that now call for attention, and also the need for a few emendations and additions in the *Anthology of Selections* from Dr Forsyth's works.

These changes, along with a fresh title, virtually make of the work a new volume. The change of title we felt was demanded by the ethos of nonconformity, as well as by the view Dr Forsyth held of the *pastoral* function of his entire work in class-room, press, and pulpit. The old title would have been too sacerdotal for his liking! On more than one occasion he spoke of the Christian pastor as Christ's curate: *Christ is the real Pastor of every real Church, and the Bishop of its minister. You are but his curate.*

The cure of souls under the Cross, was to P. T. Forsyth the grand end of both the office and work of the ministry.

GLASGOW   *H.E.*
Easter, 1966

DR P. T. FORSYTH is known to many as a theologian and a man of brilliant intellect, and the renewed interest in his work is a very cheering sign of the times. But perhaps it is not equally understood how many-sided was his personality and how wide the range of his interests; and still fewer realize that, underlying all his thinking, there was a deep faith, based on a very real personal experience of Christ's redeeming grace, and a most passionate devotion to Jesus Christ his Saviour.

For this reason Forsyth was primarily interested, not in theology as a system, but in the Gospel as redemption and life, and in its application to the manifold needs of the individual, society and the world. It is important to remember that, before he became Principal of a Theological College, he had been a preacher and pastor for twenty-five years—when, as he once put it, he was 'in a relation of life, duty and responsibility for others' (*Positive Preaching and the Modern Mind*, pp. 281–2), and all through his life he never ceased to feel the deepest concern for the souls of men and the practical bearing of the Gospel message on their lives.

This personal faith and practical concern is evident in every book, one might almost say in every paragraph, that Forsyth wrote; but it is particularly manifest in his shorter books, especially in those earlier booklets in which the keynote of all his thinking is struck, and which indeed contain *in nuce* his whole theology. These are *The Holy Father and the Living Christ, The Taste of Death and the Life of Grace*, and *Christian Perfection*. Besides these there are two books of brief compass but great suggestiveness: *The Soul of Prayer*, containing chapters written at different times in his career, and *This Life and the Next* (with the significant sub-title, 'The effect on this life of faith in another'), which was his very last work. These devotional and practical writings are not, therefore, confined to one period of his activity, but belong to every stage of his thinking and underlie all his theological work.

It was a happy inspiration which led Dr Escott to prepare an anthology of Forsyth's devotional and practical writings, revealing him, not as a theologian pure and simple, but as a director of souls. The selections are largely taken, as is only natural, from the books above named, and Dr Escott has done a valuable service in bringing to the notice of the Christian public these important and neglected works. In addition to these he has been able to draw on two sources of rather different material which throw further light on Forsyth's richly endowed mind and his intense interest in people. The first of these is the section called 'Virginibus Puerisque', where a selection is given of some of Forsyth's addresses to children, originally printed in what is actually his first book, entitled *Pulpit Parables for Young Hearers*.* The title of this book sounds rather formidable and strange to our ears, and as one reads these addresses one cannot but wonder whether the 'Young Hearers' of that day were able to digest such rich food, and still more, what the young hearers of today would make of them. But one thing at least is certain: they do reveal Forsyth's great concern for the spiritual nurture and well-being of the young people in the Church; and further, they show Forsyth, like his Master, 'setting the child in the midst' and rejoicing to give him of his very best. As we read them today, we

*See amendments in Notes on pp. xvii, xxii.

cannot but marvel at the wealth of imagination, the glowing language, and the profound spiritual truth which mark these pulpit parables.

The second source is that which is drawn upon for the final section of the book, called 'Pastoralia'. These extracts are taken from notes of addresses to his own students, made by one of them, at the week-evening services which were a notable feature of the Hackney College life during Forsyth's Principalship. These were conducted by Forsyth himself, and I have heard one of his old students say that these addresses were the best thing in his whole College course. The passages here printed reveal Forsyth's passion for the Gospel and his earnest desire that his students should become true ministers of that Gospel and in very truth 'stewards of the mysteries of God.'

These two groups of passages are especially valuable in that the original sources in both cases are inaccessible to the ordinary reader, and their inclusion gives an added value to the rich and fascinating anthology. It is to be hoped that all who read it will not only receive much personal help and inspiration, but be given a new insight into the significance of Forsyth's work and be tempted to make a closer study of his writings.

W.F.R.

1848	May 12	Born at 100 Chapel Street, Aberdeen
1859		Entered Aberdeen Grammar School.
1864	Oct.	Entered Aberdeen University.
1869		Graduated MA with first-class Honours in Classics.
1871–2		Assistant to Professor Black at Aberdeen University.
1872		Visit to Germany, Semester at Göttingen under Ritschl. Entered Hackney Theological College, Hampstead.
1874		Resigned from Hackney College.
1874–76		No records. Presumably he was living in Aberdeen.
1876		Minister of the Congregational Church, Shipley, Yorkshire. Married Miss Minna Magness.
1880		Minister of St. Thomas Square, Hackney.
1882		Visited Germany.
1885		Minister of Congregational Church, Cheetham Hill, Manchester.
1886		*Socialism and Christianity in some of their deeper Aspects.* *Pulpit Parables for Young Hearers* (with J. A. Hamilton) (Brook & Chrystal, Manchester).
1888		Minister of Clarendon Park, Leicester.
1889		*Religion in Recent Art* (Hodder &

c

		Stoughton), 2nd edition, 1911.
1893		Contributor to *Faith and Criticism*.
1894		Minister of Emmanuel Church, Cambridge. His wife's death.
1895		Granted Honorary DD, by Aberdeen University.
1896		*The Charter of the Church* (Alexander & Shepheard). *Intercessory Services for Aid in Public Worship* (John Heywood, Manchester).
		Preached the famous sermon 'Holy Father' before Assembly of Congregational Union.
		'Holy Father' published in *Christian World Pulpit*.
1897		*The Holy Father and the Living Christ* (Hodder & Stoughton). 2nd edition Independent Press, 1957.
1898	May 22	'The Happy Warrior'. A Sermon on the death of Mr Gladstone.
1898		Married Miss Bertha Ison.
1899		*Christian Perfection* (Hodder & Stoughton). *Rome, Reform and Reaction* (Hodder & Stoughton).
		Visit to America. Address on 'The Evangelical Principle of Authority' at the Decennial International Congregational Council.
		'The Atonement in Modern Religious Thought' (in *The Christian World*).
1900	May 16	'The Empire for Christ' (Sermon in the *Christian World Pulpit*).
		Contributed to *The Atonement in Modern Religious Thought*.
1901		Principal, Hackney College, London.

1901		*The Taste of Death and the Life of Grace.*
1902		*Holy Christian Empire*, a Sermon.
1903		'The New Congregationalism and the New Testament Congregationalism' (in the *Examiner*).
1905		Chairman of the Congregational Union of England and Wales.
	May 9	*A Holy Church the Moral Guide of Society*, an Address delivered in the City Temple (published by the Congregational Union of England and Wales). Reissued by Independent Press in 1962 as part of *The Church, the Gospel and Society.*
	Oct. 10	*The Grace of the Gospel as the Moral Authority in the Church*, an Address in the Coliseum, Leeds (published by the Congregational Union of England and Wales). Reissued by Independent Press in 1962 as part of *The Church, the Gospel and Society.*
	Oct.	'The Evangelical Churches and the Higher Criticism' (*Contemporary Review*, pp. 574–99).
	Oct.	'Some Christian Aspects of Evolution' (*The London Quarterly Review*, pp. 209–39).
1907		Visit to America. Lyman Beecher Lectures at Yale University.
		Positive Preaching and the Modern Mind (Hodder & Stoughton). 2nd edition Independent Press, 1949.
1908		*Missions in State and Church* (Hodder & Stoughton). *Socialism, the Church and the Poor* (Hodder & Stoughton).

1908	*The Inspiration and Authority of Holy Scripture* (with Monro Gibson). 'The Distinctive Thing in Christian Experience' (in the *Hibbert Journal*). 'Christ at the Gate', 'The Majesty of Christ' (in the *Christian World Pulpit*).
1909	*The Cruciality of the Cross* (Hodder & Stoughton). New edition Independent Press, 1948. *Pastoralia* (previously unpublished, cf. Part Eight of the Anthology). *The Person and Place of Jesus Christ* (Hodder & Stoughton and Independent Press). 4th edition, 1930, 5th edition, 1946. 'The Insufficiency of Social Righteousness as a Moral Ideal' (*Hibbert Journal*).
1910	*The Work of Christ* (Hodder & Stoughton). 2nd edition Independent Press, 1938; 3rd edition in preparation. *The Power of Prayer* (with Dora Greenwell) (Hodder & Stoughton).
June-July	'Calvinism and Capitalism' (*Contemporary Review*).
1911	Dean of the Faculty of Theology, London University. *Christ on Parnassus* (Hodder & Stoughton). 2nd edition Independent Press, 1959. Contributed 'Christ and the Christian Principle' to *London Theological Studies*.
1912	*Faith, Freedom and the Future* (Hodder &

Stoughton). New edition Independent Press, 1955.

Marriage, Its Ethic and Religion (Hodder & Stoughton).

1913   *The Principle of Authority* (Hodder & Stoughton). New edition Independent Press, 1952.

1915   *Theology in State and Church* (Hodder & Stoughton). 'The Preaching of Jesus and the Gospel of Christ' in the *Expositor*, April, May, July, Aug., Oct., and Nov.

1916   *The Christian Ethic of War* (Longmans Green & Co.).

The Justification of God (Duckworth & Co.). 2nd edition Independent Press, 1957.

The Soul of Prayer (The Epworth Press). 2nd edition Independent Press, 1949.

'The Spiritual Needs in the Churches' (in the *Christian World Pulpit*).

1917   *The Church and the Sacraments* (Longmans Green & Co.) (with H. T. Andrews). New edition Independent Press, 1947.

Reunion and Recognition, pamphlet (Congregational Union of England & Wales). 2nd edition Independent Press, 1952.

1918   *The Roots of a World Commonwealth*, pamphlet (Hodder & Stoughton).

Congregationalism and Reunion (London). 2nd edition Independent Press, 1952.

This Life and the Next (Macmillan &

Co.). 2nd edition Independent Press, 1946.

1921   Nov. 11   P. T. Forsyth died in London.

SINCE the appearance of this book in 1948 some interesting facts have come to light with regard to the early years of Dr Forsyth's life. He was born at 100 Chapel Street, Old Aberdeen. His father, Isaac Forsyth, set up business in that city, first as a bookseller, and later as a canvasser of books. When these occupations proved to be economically inadequate he joined the postal service. Peter's mother buttressed the domestic finances by taking student lodgers.

On the completion of his university course (crowned with many honours but also interrupted by a long period of illness) young Forsyth became assistant to Dr Black in the Department of Humanity of King's College, Aberdeen. Hence his visit to Germany and first pastorate have required to be post-dated by a few years. Moreover, his first writing was not *Pulpit Parables* but a tract on Socialism. And perhaps his earliest formative theological influences were in Aberdeen (and not in England) under the ministry of Thomas Gilfillan of Blackfriars Street Congregational Church (now Skene Street) and subsequently under A. M. Fairbairn.

An Appraisement

The Reanimation of Forsyth

'THAT body once was a temple of the Holy Ghost, and is now become a small quantity of Christian dust. *But I shall see it reanimated.*' Thus Izaak Walton finishes his portrait—one of the best biographies in English—of his friend and pastor John Donne. He was speaking of the immortal hope, but his words were prophetic in another sense; recent years have seen a resurgence of interest in the works of Donne, as poet and preacher. This *reanimation* of the seventeenth-century writer has exercised an influence on modern poets and thinkers.

Walton's words could be applied in this latter sense to another great theologian and preacher, Peter Taylor Forsyth, in some ways not dissimilar to that earlier *agonistes* of the spirit, and like him known chiefly through a brief yet breathing Memoir. Both men are pathologists of the soul, sounding its deeps, as well as exploring the deeper depths of grace. Both are masters of English prose and write in the sweat of wrestling with massive ideas. Each is a writer of strong sinew, a Vulcan beating out truths, and neither is an artist by intention, though there are rare jewels among the sparks that fly from their anvils. Both men bend a heavy knowledge to serve the Gospel that holds them to their sinew-splitting work.

Donne is more self-revealing and introspective, more concerned to anatomize the individual soul than Forsyth. It is easier to discern a thread of spiritual autobiography in the Englishman than in the Scot. We see Donne agonizing with the Angel. But in Forsyth,

I

due largely to his Scottish reticence and the late date at which he became a writer, the celestial battle is over and won; the heavenly combatant has left him, albeit with his thigh of pride put out. He has the victory. His Jabbok, like the red deaths of the classical drama, happens, so to say, off-stage; but the curtain be it never so heavy cannot drown the thuds and heavy breathing of the antagonists. It is clear, as we read between the lines of these thinly-veiled autobiographical passages, that Forsyth experienced in the work of the ministry a second conversion. He is fond of the figure of the *wrestler* who is hardly saved in the conflict. He has the evangelical's preference for the twice-born man.

Another writer* accounts for the reanimation of Forsyth. 'Forsyth', he says, 'anticipated the modern disillusionment with the doctrines of inevitable progress and the innate perfectibility of human nature. He withstood the illegitimate extension of biological theories of evolution into non-biological areas. He indicated the Nemesis of liberalism in an historical religion.' These insights, far in advance of his day, have been confirmed by the havoc of two world wars and his writings now 'come home to men's business and bosoms' with the force of divine truth.

Moreover, the crisis of our age has made his commentary on the New Testament thought-world intelligible and congenial. When British scholars were obsessed with the complexity of the New Testament, Forsyth was reaching the heart of its unity, concentrating, not on the analysis of its documents, but on the centre of its message, on what we today call the *kerygma*. 'Criticism is the handmaid of the Gospel—downstairs. The critical study of Scripture is at its best, and the higher criticism is at its highest, when it passes from

*T. R. Meadley, *Congregational Quarterly*, October 1946.

being analytic and becomes *synthetic*. And the synthetic principle in the Bible is the Gospel. The analysis of the Bible must serve the history of Grace. The synthetic critic is not the scholar but the theologian. The Book is a witness not of man's historical religion, but of God's historical redemption.' It is difficult to realize that these words, so modern in tone, were written as early as 1905. There is little in the 'discoveries' of Dibelius, Rawlinson, and Dodd, and the *Formgeschichte* school that is not found *in germ* in the writings of Forsyth.

The Mystery of his 'Conversion'

AN interesting study might be made of the effect of temperament on philosophical or theological thinking. As temperament is, to some extent, a *resultant* of the union of hereditary, social, geographical, and cultural factors, to know something about these factors should help us towards a more sympathetic understanding of a man's thought and general view of life. Peter Taylor Forsyth was born at Aberdeen in 1848, of Aberdeenshire and Highland peasant stock. This commingling of blood perhaps accounts in his make-up for that strange but happy mixture of Highland poetry and Aberdonian practicality. United in him are the militant righteousness of the evangelical, the Celtic love of 'Faery', and the Highlander's second sight—in theology.

His parents were born and nurtured in the mountainous marches of Banffshire and the county of Aberdeen—regions of grey skies, great silences, stubborn glebes—where sometimes a cruel climate means late or ruined harvests, and always unremitting toil. Such a

3

habitat hardly fosters the genial virtues, or feeds an easy optimism, or begets a mystical piety. It is more likely to produce *askesis* than *ekstasis*. Where life from day to day is an endless conflict with land and elements, within a limited range of relationships, it is not surprising that the *will* rather than the affections should loom large in religious thought and practice. Beetling hills shrouded in mist—loud silences—long absences from companionship—these are the natural background of speculative thought and religious mystery, making *holiness* rather than love the predominant note of thought and conduct, and affording a native nursery for Calvinism. Forsyth inherited this legacy, but it was lightened by a more distant endowment of Celtic passion and imagination, and subsequently broadened by the influence of the university culture of a seaport town.

His parents settled in the city of Aberdeen and it was there Peter was born. Probably they shared the ambition of Scottish parents of those days, that their boy should wear the coveted toga of the University. The Scot has a flair for adventure. He has won place among explorers, settlers, and pioneer-missionaries, and when the physical energy needed for these vigorous undertakings would seem to be denied, he has set his face toward some gleaming peak of *mental* endeavour. So it was with young Forsyth. He had it in him—and the necessary parental pride and support were not wanting —to be a leader in this field of adventure.

At the Grammar School, and later in the University of Aberdeen, he earned a high place in scholarship. Caught up in the fascinating scientific analysis of the Bible—congenial to a classical and philosophic mind like his own—he went, after graduation, to Germany to study under Albrecht Ritschl. Then followed a course

4

of study at Hackney Theological College, Hampstead, and in 1876 we find him in his first pastorate, as minister of the Congregational Church, Shipley, Yorkshire—by all accounts an out-and-out 'modernist', regarded with suspicion by the pillars of the Church. But in the course of his ministry here and elsewhere, a great change came over him. Accounting for this strange reorientation, he says, 'There was a time when I was interested in the first degree with purely scientific criticism. Bred among academic scholarship of the classics and philosophy, I carried these habits to the Bible, and I found in the subject a new fascination, in proportion as the stakes were so much higher. But, fortunately for me, I was not condemned to the mere scholar's cloistered life. I could not treat the matter as an academic quest. I was in a relation of life, duty, and responsibility for others. I could not contemplate conclusions without asking how they would affect these people and my word to them in doubt, death, grief, or repentance . . . It also pleased God, by the revelation of his holiness and grace, which the great theologians taught me to find in the Bible, to bring home to me my sin in a way that submerged all the school questions in weight, urgency, and poignancy.' Reading between these lines we think that like Owen and Goodwin, two of his favourite 'great theologians' and like Donne, whom we have seen he resembles, Forsyth realized that his 'hydroptique immoderate desire of humane learning and languages' could bring no true peace, and had nothing deep and real enough to help him minister to souls diseased.

He had probably raised his voice with others against the old beliefs, but he saw now that the ancient orthodoxies had a power to heal the hurt of the people denied the systems which were usurping their place.

5

From bondage to the old beliefs
You say our rescue must begin,
But I want refuge from my griefs,
And saving from my sin.

Thus it was with Forsyth, as with others before him and since his day, the fruit of the tree of knowledge was as an apple of Sodom bitter to his taste. Henceforth there was only one way open to him—the crucifixion of the very culture that he had prized almost above everything else. His rich and varied gifts of mind and imagination were laid from now on at the foot of the Cross. There is autobiography in the words he addressed to the Congregational Union of England and Wales, at Leeds, 10th October 1905. He is speaking of the old orthodoxies: 'They had not arrived,' he says, 'as the poetic sermon, the sermon of genial ethic and kindly piety, the social sermon, the literary sermon, the Tennyson sermon, and the Browning, and the Whittier worst of all. I have heard many of them, *and I have preached more*. Oh, do not tell me, for I know, of the romance of passion, the witchery of beauty, and the stately measure of classic grace. I have lived in that land of milk and honey and generous wine. But a curse is on us that these cannot lift. God be merciful to us sinners.' These are words of a twice-born man smashed and made anew by the hands of the Divine Potter!

Doubtless referring to his youthful days of theological liberalism, and contrasting them with his later days of mature faith, he once said to his students at Hackney College, 'God takes the morning star out of the sky of youthful idealism that he may give it back to us for a possession when we enter upon the full life of Christian faith.'

JOHN OMAN distinguishes the true from the false prophet: 'The false prophet is a shell gathering up and echoing the spirit of the age; the true prophet is no echo of the moods and passions of his age, but a living voice declaring what is its true lesson.'* That describes the mission of Forsyth to his age, and to our own. He belongs to the prophetic type of theologian, not the formal, and his 'oracles' do not lend themselves to analysis of sources or to systematization. In him we find all the splendid 'failings' of the prophet—incoherences, obsessions, one-sidednesses, enthusiasms. He has the emotional verve, the horror of systematization which stamp the prophetic attitude and utterance. Any attempt to suggest the depth and sweep of his thinking with the aid of editorial scissors and paste is foredoomed to failure. He is one of our few theological writers which no anthology can at all adequately represent. What he wrote about the Hebrew mentality might be said with few reservations about his own: 'The Hebrew imagination was quick, mobile, and realistic, not calm, intuitive, and constructive. They were a passionate, direct, and strong-willed people, who regarded the world entirely in relation to their own place in it. They could not examine it at arm's length, so to speak. They never thought how it would look in a picture, or how it might be scientifically expressed. They had neither pictorial taste nor scientific curiosity. It was a personal, not a theoretic standard they had for things. Their religion . . . was one based on personality, or personal qualities and relations. They had no theories

Grace and Personality, p. 9.

7

of the universe. It was all the result of the fiat of a supreme will. There is a theology, and above all a teleology, but no system, in the Old Testament. They did not desire to examine the concatenation of things, but their destination .... Everything was the immediate result of a will, and everything had a purpose. This will and this purpose it was the business of their great spokesman, the prophet, to see and foresee, and to expound them with all the resources of an oratory more full of force than balance.'* Yes, Forsyth's mind was more Hebraic than Greek; he was a prophet, not a systematizer. The passage not only describes the writer's own peculiarities and genius, but epitomizes too the orientation of the present day movement towards theological realism.

Gladstone's dictum that the orator 'receives from his audience in a vapour what he returns in a flood' is as true of the prophetic teacher as of the political leader. We shall try to show to what extent Forsyth, in so many ways a lone explorer in the region of the spirit, was indebted to his age. Except for a few expressions of such indebtedness, there is little to help us trace the sources of his ideas. The absence of documentation, alongside a lack of system in his writings, has made some question Forsyth's scholarship. The truth is he belongs to a kind of scholarship—unfortunately at a discount—the prophetic, creative kind in which the wheat of reading, meditation, and thought gleaned from many fields, is milled, leavened by prayer, and becomes in the process a bread of life. We do not therefore detract from his work as writer and thinker if we should admit that one cannot classify him with the readiness that pleases the editor of theological textbooks. But as absolute insularity from the atmosphere of his age

*Christ on Parnassus, p. 59.

8

would have been impossible, the student of his books will find the influences of nineteenth-century philosophy and theology, and overhear from time to time echoes of the English poets whom he so deeply loved and understood.

His daughter tells us that about one-third of the books in his library were in German and that he kept abreast with thought in that country by the regular reading of its periodic literature. This information, along with Forsyth's own admission of indebtedness to the Germans, has most probably fostered the idea that his *chief* affiliations as a theological thinker must be looked for in that direction. There can be no doubt that he owed a great deal to Hegel, Ritschl, Kähler, and Zahn, and something to Ihmels, Schaeder, and Schlatter. He was perhaps the first theologian in this country to perceive the importance of Kierkegaard. He quotes him in *The Work of Christ*, and in *The Principle of Authority* he says: 'There is no greater division within religion than that between Emerson and Kierkegaard, between a religion that but concentrates the optimism of clean youth, and that which hallows the tragic note and deals with a world *sick unto death*.'

Pascal, too, was a favourite of his. He is fond of quoting the Frenchman's memorable saying: 'Christ is crucified to the world's end.' Forsyth advised his students to throw George Macdonald aside and read Pascal. Macdonald was a large in Rite Taylor's book looked after his book

But there were English influences too. The greatest, because an early one, was Frederick Denison Maurice who gave him a love for theology, 'to which he returned later after some dalliance with literary and aesthetic interests, to make the permanent and fruitful union of his life'. Like Maurice he always felt as a theologian, thought as a theologian, wrote as a theologian. All

9

things were to his mind connected with theology and subordinate to it. Whether he is writing for children, or the philosopher, or even the aesthete, the Cross is Forsyth's abiding obsession. From Maurice too he learnt 'that whether it were Nature or the Bible that was being studied, it should be studied patiently, humbly, and self-effacingly with a view not to placing our own interpretations upon it, but to learning the lessons which it has to teach.'

His conception of faith too was like Maurice's, who writes in a sermon on the Creed: '. . . any definite notion about faith, any effort to put it forward bodily, was alien from the spirit of primitive times, however many instances of the experiment be actually found, however many the critics of later times may have imagined. *The "believe" is really lost in him who is believed. The faith goes out of the "I" into the object. It does not try to realize itself, apart from the one or the other.*' If the reader wishes to see how Forsyth's teaching resembles the older theologian's, he need only compare the above passage with the section in the Anthology on 'The Perfection of Faith'.

Writers on Forsyth have made much—too much we believe—of his antipathy to Mysticism. Consequently they have concealed from view a very real mystical vein in his work. He taught, and truly, that nothing so subjective as pietism could be a Gospel for a Church. He saw the necessity of a positive objective Word of God as the bed-rock of the Church's life and preaching. He had the evangelical's horror of mere states and feelings as substitutes for the mighty fact of God's redeeming deed. A keen student of Church history, he knew the danger of placing authority on anything so fickle and indeterminate as *spirit*, rather than on Christ's atoning work on the Cross. What God has *done* and not what man *feels* is the only real authority for a Church.

At the same time, there is ample proof that Forsyth nourished his soul on the writings of the mystics. In a letter to William Robertson Nicoll, in which he expresses his appreciation of Nicoll's little treatise on mystical theology, *The Garden of Nuts*, he says: 'I have misrepresented myself in having left the impression you get as to my attitude to mysticism. Pietism I confess to disliking, but I love the mystics. Bernard is my favourite saint and his "Canticles" an old delight. I only object to mysticism used as the sufficient basis of religious certainty for a whole Church. I seem to see many of our ministers going to seed or to slush on it, and exercising a vague ministry which becomes vaguer and feebler still as it filters down through their people. I fancy they think it easier—though to the true mystic it is certainly not so.'

Forsyth takes his stand with 'the true mystic,' by which he means the evangelical mystic. Adolf Deissmann draws the distinction between two kinds of mystical experience, which he calls 'acting' and 'reacting' mysticism. The 'acting' mystic he describes as the person who wishes to explore the unseen for his own benefit, who belongs to a spiritual aristocracy, so to speak, and desires the monopoly of spiritual insight. The 'reacting' mystic, on the other hand, like Paul and Augustine and the great spiritual geniuses of the Church, does not search for God, but responds or 'reacts' to a God who has initiated the search, and made himself known through revelation. The *moral* and not the metaphysical is therefore the motive of this type of mysticism. To this latter category Forsyth belongs. Some of his greatest passages—particularly his perorations—are, we think, among the finest evangelical mystical utterances in the English language.

Two of his little volumes, amply represented by quotation in the anthology, *Christian Perfection* and *The Soul of Prayer*, remind us of William Law's books with almost the same titles. Forsyth must have read deeply in Law, and in certain places repeats, unconsciously, almost the words of the eighteenth-century director of souls.

Through Law, or through Hegel, he seems to have assimilated some of the ideas of Jacob Boehme, whom Hegel acclaimed as the Father of German Philosophy, and who has had a profound influence on English religious thought. Boehme's philosophy can be apprehended only by living it, and accordingly the *will* is the radical force in man and in God. This practical and experiential side of the teaching of the German mystic would appeal to Forsyth. Boehme, moreover, lays peculiar stress on the duality of wills. The central point of his philosophy is that all manifestation necessitates opposition. Prayer with him, as in the teaching of Forsyth, is a battle, a conflict of *wills*. Forsyth never wearies of stressing the *activity* of prayer. We are exhorted over and over again to work hard in the life of prayer. He reminds us that Jesus *prayed in an agony*: 'We must pray even to tears if need be. Our co-operation with God is our receptivity; but it is an *active*, and laborious receptivity, an importunity that drains our strength away if it do not tap the sources of the Strength Eternal.' In another place he says: 'We turn to an active Giver; therefore we go into action. . . . If God has a controversy with Israel, Israel must *wrestle* with God.'

Another echo of Boehme's teaching in the pages of Forsyth is the idea that life springs out of the co-operation of opposites. He probably derived it from Hegel, but it was originally Boehme's insight. In *Christian Perfection* (pp. 14-16) Forsyth finds a place for the dark, earthy passions in the psychology of redemption: 'All life, it has been said, is the holding down of a dark, wild, elemental nature at our base, which is most useful, like steam, under due pressure. So with sin and its mastery by faith. The pressure from below drives us to God and the communion with God by faith keeps it always below. The outward pressure of nature, and even of perverted nature in man develops in him through God a power which converts, controls, utilizes, and exalts nature. It is doubtful if real holiness is quite possible to people who have no "nature" in them, no passion, no flavour of the good brown earth. Take away that elemental rage from below and you make faith a blanched inept thing. You have no more than quietist piety, passive religion, perfect in sound happy natures as an enjoyment, but very imperfect as a power. Faith, in a true sense, is all-sufficient, because it brings a rest which is itself power, force, will. It is the offspring of God's power and man's; it is not the mere occupation of man by God, which as often means suppression as inspiration.'

This section on Forsyth's affiliations would be incomplete without reference to Dora Greenwell and the Puritans. William Robertson Nicoll confessed that he had learnt more theology from Dora Greenwell than from any other teacher. It was he who suggested that Miss Greenwell's essay *Prayer* should be bound up with one by Forsyth to form the lovely volume *The Power of Prayer* which Nicoll edited in his *Little Books of Religion* in 1910. Nicoll with his penetrating eye saw the affinity of thought and attitude between the two writers. And it is not surprising to find Forsyth himself expressing indebtedness to Dora Greenwell in the opening words of his own contribution to the book: '. . . I should like by a word to express my sense of the deep spiritual insight that pervades all her work—the deeper as she nears the centre. She is a great expositor of the Cross and its poignancy. And her vision is as delicate as it is deep. She has the saintly note. . . .'

Doubtless Forsyth, like other young intellectuals, was early fascinated by the writings of Dora Greenwell. Her point of view exhibits a broadness and catholicity seldom seen in religious writing. She addresses the intellect no less than the affections. Her books appeal to those who have a cultivated sense of religious truth. They unite social and mental culture with spiritual insight. It would have been strange therefore if a mind of Forsyth's varied and creative character had not come under the spell of so virile and original a writer. We are inclined to think it did so, and that her books (so centred in the Cross like his own) were a formative influence in the years of silence when he was finding his way to his soul's magnetic north. The Cross which each held with tenacious grasp, and which held them both, is the central passion of the two writers, though there is less dogma in Miss Greenwell than in the more speculative Scottish thinker. The fact of the Cross—though in some ways enigmatic—was sufficient for her; but Forsyth must think through to a theology of the Atonement. The point we wish to make here is that the statement often made that Forsyth was a solitary figure in English theology is not quite true. In Dora Greenwell he had had a kindred spirit in the field before him, and men like Dale, Denney, and Bruce were in sympathy with him too.

Dora Greenwell's last prose work was written when Forsyth was barely thirty, but many of her books were reprinted during the last quarter of the nineteenth-century, and there is reason to believe that he read and pondered them. She always put into words the silent, unventured convictions of serious minds, and scattered along her perhaps too richly-loaded pages are hints and suggestions each of which would furnish a spiritual spring-board for an alert brain like Forsyth's. Accordingly, it is not surprising to find in Forsyth some of Dora Greenwell's ideas, namely, the centrality of an objective Atonement, a keen sense of the value of Protestantism, along with a dauntless Catholicity, the conception of prayer as a conflict of wills, in which man's will can also act on God's, belief in the *synthetic principle* as the real clue to the meaning of the Bible, and the idea of the solidarity of mankind in sin and the necessity of a cosmic, and not merely an individual, redemption.

Such ideas, alien to most of the theology of the nineteenth-century, these two great expositors of the Cross and its poignancy held in common.

There is indirect evidence that Forsyth's mind worked on the books of Gore, Moberly, and McLeod Campbell. And we have to record the sadly short-lived influence of Dale, and the acknowledged indebtedness to Fairbairn. Then there is Newman, whose influence has not been given sufficient emphasis in the study of Forsyth. As early as 1905 Forsyth was working on the problem of Authority. His Autumnal Address to the Congregational Union in October of that year had for its theme 'The Grace of the Gospel as the Moral Authority in the Church.' He says that in many churches we have no due sense of the majesty of God, and do not stand in the real presence. We give people interests and sympathies, but not moral authority: 'Do we give them what Rome gives in her way—what overawes the soul—a real authority and guide for life?' Forsyth was faced by Newman's problem, though he solved it differently. He saw the same demon of liberalism but he fought it in another way.

Justice has not been done to the influence of the Puritan theologians on the work of Forsyth. His writings, for the most part, are cast in the form of sermons or lectures not in systematic treatises. This is true of practically all his books which preceded the first World War; it was only in the war years, when presumably he had leisure for writing and was less concerned with practical work, that his books became academic, his style concentrated, and his exposition systematic. This is most important. It confirms what has been said earlier, that Forsyth was no theorist in theology, working out a system *in vacuo* out of relation to men and their needs. He was essentially a preacher; his books were really printed sermons; and his message is, therefore, always living and warm, close to the life of his audience and the problems of his age. Thus in matter and method his writings were of the Puritan heritage. He was forwarding the tradition of the great days of Independency and was following the example of his predecessors, men like Goodwin, Owen, and Robinson.

Often Forsyth expresses admiration for 'his Puritans'. Like them, he had a *theologia pectoris*. He knew that the true interpreter of the Bible is neither the higher criticism nor an authoritative Church but the evangelical experience of an awakened heart. In one of his books he writes of the theology of these men in the following terms: 'Their type of religion was rooted in a positive and experimental soil, in the evangelical experience, and from there it grew. The Gospel was fixed, and not only as the keystone of a system but as a living genetic centre. . . . It gave the theology a living soul. It set it in motion with a personal thrill. It made the theology passionate, as the projection and confession of life created anew in the Holy Spirit. Its treatises were conceived, delivered, and published as sermons. Theology was not an abstract science which might be pursued by a speculative calculus with comparative personal indifference; it was a transcript of personal faith, developed in a living company of saints. . . . Theology became capable of being preached, because it was a living thing, a life's confession. Like a great epic it was first lived.'

All that is equally true of Forsyth's own work; and the words which, a moment later, he uses in speaking of Goodwin's writings, seem applicable to many of his own pages: 'They not only tingle, they soar; and they come home with a beauty and poignancy of spiritual truth which makes them, even after they are read, ingredients in one's own spiritual life.'

His Style

WE turn to a side of Forsyth's work which has received little if any attention—his mastery of English prose. There are passages of sheer beauty shining like jewels in the pages of his books, which as literature deserve a place in a selection of English prose of the nineteenth-century. We venture to say that there was a time in his life when he aspired to literary distinction. He read widely in all branches of literature, and was a keen student of aesthetics; one great painter acclaimed him the best commentator on his artistic aims.

In the earliest writings we possess, the *Parables*, we see him experimenting with words, with rhythms and cadences which remind us of the George Gissing of

Ryecroft and the *Ionian Sea.* But this self-conscious phase in Forsyth's apprenticeship to letters came to an abrupt end with something like a new conversion. The whole man, as he himself implies in passages of thinly-veiled autobiography, was smashed to pieces and made anew. So was his style. Crucified, dead, and buried, it rose again in newness of life, powerful, persuasive, beautiful. No longer was it an instrument held at arm's length, but an agent of his redeemed personality; and he shed it, as a man might shed his life's blood, in the cause of the Gospel. *Le style c'est l'homme*—was never more true than in the case of Forsyth.

After this religious renaissance his style became more natural. It reminds us now of the Gissing of the realistic passages in *Demos, New Grub Street,* and *Thyrza.* It has lost its pristine prettiness; it is real, glowing, strong, and fits close as a glove to the theological realism. Everywhere there are passages like etchings. And now and again the realism is relieved by a touch of romance, or by some mystic vision.

As we read such passages we feel that what his daughter wrote of their cost to the writer in nervous energy can be no overstatement. Virtue went out of him as he wrote. His books are indeed—on a literary estimate (and how he would have hated this)—the life blood of a master spirit.

It has been remarked (and by one hardly fitted to appreciate the theological insights of Forsyth) that his use of quotation from the poets is always happy, choice, unhackneyed. This is true on the comparatively few occasions when he makes direct citation. What has been said of his use of the ideas of theologians and philosophers might be repeated of the way he employs the treasure trove of literature and art. He does not so much *import* these into his writing, as *transfuse* them—

to adopt a vitalistic term—into his personality; and when we discern them again on his pages they appear as new creations. Should the reader wish to study this *assimilative* genius of Forsyth, he need only refer to the Anthology, tracing to their sources half-concealed literary echoes. Forsyth was one of the few men of his age who had a sympathetic understanding of the main trends of European literature.

Yet he is not an 'easy' writer. It is not sufficient to 'read' his books; they must be studied, or rather *felt*. J. G. Stevenson's stricture on their style, 'fireworks in a fog,' has been shared by others, J. H. Jowett, George Jackson, and A. S. Peake, to mention but a few of his more famous critics. But if we cannot understand Forsyth, the fault usually is in ourselves, hardly ever on his side. This for two reasons. The first is connected with the peculiar literary ethos of our time. The rapid development of science since the seventeenth-century has had as its corollary the framing of a scientific language. It began with John Wilkins and the founders of the Royal Society, who wished to find a simple, lucid and logical speech for the purpose of scientific description. So far, so good. But when this denuded speech was taken over by the man in the street, and used to convey the meaning of the complexities of human experience, it determined a literal-mindedness, a tendency to see in words only one unique and un-emotive reference.

Today physical accuracy has become almost the sole criterion of truth; metaphor, rhythm and paradox have to apologize for their very existence. We are becoming blind to the appeal of poetry and prophetic speech, and losing the capacity to hear and understand overtones and undertones of meaning in them. Now Forsyth would seem to be a reactionary. His use of language has more affinity with Donne's than Tillotson's. His prose speaks not only to the eye and brain, but to the gamut of the senses—to the whole man, for it is in essence *faith-language*, the speech used by faith when it thinks and utters. Consequently his language is sometimes more akin to music than mathematics. Like Herbert, Vaughan, Jeremy Taylor and Lancelot Andrewes, Forsyth is dealing with transcendent ideas. The thought of Redemption, for example, so central in all his works, was not 'an abstract counter to be manipulated in men's minds according to the rules of grammar and logic; it was a motive, a source of action and inspiration, and its meaning could come only by repetitions, sensuous images, sound patterns, paradoxes and ambiguity.' A simple style was impossible, as he himself confesses. It would have been dishonest, a deliberate distortion of the complexity and richness of Christian experience. Hence the habilitation of one of our foremost theological thinkers is hindered by the fact that he is out of *rapport* with the literary ethos of the age.

Forsyth reminds us in his use of language of another writer who has come to his own in recent years, Gerald Manley Hopkins. He too was as alien to the idiom of his day as to its spiritual blindness and lethargy. And his uncommon idiom was no pose, but the expression of a personal experience. Experience and utterance are as closely related in Hopkins as in Forsyth. It is this fact that constitutes their resemblance. Hopkins rediscovered in spiritual fellowship with Shakespeare and the 'metaphysicals' the evocative power of words and rhythms that had been clipped off by the sharp-edged scientific scissors. Like Forsyth he has his difficult idiosyncrasies and irritating subtleties of style. What has been said of his literary 'lapses' might equally have been written in defence of Forsyth's 'obscurities': '[The] variation in response (to Hopkins' style) is not primarily a matter of *literary* judgement, though it may rationalize itself as such. It depends upon the degree to which the reader is ready to respond to the exceptional and in some ways over-taut intensity of Hopkins' *experience*. Those who have complained that he strove against the genius of the English language have really been complaining that he strained unwarrantably against the measure of human experience which they wish to accept.'

So we are carried along to the second reason for the modern failure to understand Forsyth. It is not just a matter of *ethos*: his *experience* is strange to us too. Hopkins' language was an attempt to adumbrate a soul-shattering experience, and to understand the style one must be in sympathy with the poet. The same applies to Forsyth. 'All words, even the greatest,' he says, 'are made from the dust and spring from our sandy passions, earthly needs, and fleeting thoughts; and they are hard to stretch to the measure of eternal things without breaking under us somewhere.' It is not surprising that an age without the evangelical experience should be lacking in sympathy for one of its most evangelical writers.

> *Wer den Dichter will verstehen*
> *Muss in Dichters Lande gehen;*

or, as Forsyth said: 'The merchantmen of these goodly pearls must be seekers; and without even divers they cannot be had.'

Forsyth and Barthianism

A SCOTTISH theologian of my acquaintance, while on a visit to Ireland, fell in with an Irish minister who had quoted Forsyth to Karl Barth, and heard the great man of Basel retort: 'If Forsyth had not said what he said when he said it, I would have said he was quoting me.'

Forsyth has been called 'a Barthian before Barth.' Any label, least of all this one, does scant justice to his originality and genius. It is absurd to class in the category of disciple a man who preached and wrote—and these remarkably—when his 'master' was still a boy at school. Barth's first important work, the *Commentary on the Epistle to the Romans*, was published in 1918 when the writer was only thirty-two years old. In the same year Forsyth gave us his *last* book. The very contemporaneity of the tragic situation which Barth sought to meet in his theology has given to the Continental theologian a significance and stature denied his precursor in the same field who, while possessing all Barth's insights, lived and wrote at a time when apparently there was little in the human scene to reinforce and substantiate them. Barth's book was like a volcano—'a bomb dropped on the theological playgrounds of Europe.' But Forsyth, in comparatively halcyon days, had made Barth's rediscovery of the Word of God, and he had dropped his bombs, albeit in a sea of indifference where, in the nature of things, they could not explode with the same shattering violence.

Should we, however, decide to award the laurel to the Swiss for his commanding height, the Scot deserves precedence for his greater width of outlook and culture.

There is a humanity and compassion about Forsyth which seem to be lacking in the Continental theologian. Forsyth never forgets humanity in his zeal for the Word. He nowhere

> *Barters the things*
> *Bound to the earth, besmirchèd underlings.*

This Barth does. Some disquieting discontinuity there is, even in Forsyth, between Nature and Revelation, but the cleavage is not perhaps so decisive, dark, and grim as with Barth. Human life still has its grandeur and Art its glimmerings of divine truth.

All the emotions, all the relationships of hearth and business come within the Kingdom. God, who is thought of chiefly in terms of holiness, is presented as turning to the earth with intensest pity. This bracing breeze from Galilee blowing through Forsyth's pages endears them to us. He has the thunder and lightning of Barth, though less fiercely and less clamantly, but there is also the still small voice of one who would speak words of comfort to his fellows.

We recall a passage by one whose voice alas is now silent and whose wise pen is laid aside: 'How I give thanks for Karl Barth and his trumpet voice and his faithful testimony; he has been a prophet in these past years! It is inevitable, however, that anyone so pusillanimous and hesitant and sluggish-hearted as myself should be discomfited in his presence. Yet, somehow, I feel that God himself will not be quite so extreme to mark what is done amiss, or, if that is not quite the way to put it, let me say that my sympathy is all with the children of Israel who stayed at the foot of the mountain while Moses (imagined as slightly like Dr Barth) ascended into the thick darkness on the mountain top; or, if even this be regarded as slightly disrespectful to Moses or Dr Barth, I will amend and say that to study

Dr Barth's theology is to be in church with the notes of the great organ rolling round the pillars and the blood-red light shining through the stained glass of the Judgement Scene above the altar; it is awe-inspiring, almost too much for flesh and blood; but every now and then I get a peep through the church porch, for the great door has been left conveniently open, and it is warm and sunny outside, and the butterflies, especially the little blue ones, are fluttering about the bedstraw and the clover which are (but, I suppose, ought not to be) in the churchyard, and the birds are singing very quietly but very happily. I would not escape from the terrors of Mount Sinai, but I want to "consider the lilies," too, and join the song of the birds, and I think that, when the organ stops (thank God for that solemn overwhelming music!) I shall find that "the sparrow hath found her a house and the swallow a nest where she may lay her young, even thy altars, O Lord of Hosts, my King and my God".' (John A. Hutton).

To put it in a nutshell, Peter Taylor Forsyth kept the balance which marks most English theological thinking; like Jesus he loved the lily and was faithful to the Cross.

Forsyth and the Cure of Souls

THE TITLE of this revised book was originally *Peter Taylor Forsyth: Director of Souls*. The word 'director' has sacerdotal associations which were anathema to a protestant mind such as Forsyth's. Hence in this new edition we have amended the title to *P. T. Forsyth and the Cure of Souls*. Yet there are many in the ministry of the Churches today who owe their devotional habits to his personal *direction*, and the quiet talks he gave weekly to his students in the College chapel (cf. 'Pastoralia'). *Christian Perfection* and *The Soul of Prayer*— two little classics of the spiritual life—have done the same thing for others who never heard his voice. He was indeed a protestant director pointing the soul to God; and for many the pondering of his pages has been in the nature of a second conversion. This more intimate devotional side of his rich nature has not received its due consideration. His own heart-wrestling with God in thought and prayer was the source of those grand theological insights of which we have been speaking. 'The bane,' he writes, 'of so much theology, old and new, is that it has been denuded of prayer and prepared in a vacuum.'

But Forsyth was never chiefly concerned with *souls in their privacy* like Thomas à Kempis and the writers of some Catholic manuals of devotion. His real affinity was, as we have seen, with the Puritans and his chief concern with the *world* soul awry, dark, despairing, unreconciled. This universal sweep in his devotional speaking and writing sets him almost by himself. He was more a director of the *Soul* than of souls. His devotional, like his more scholarly theological work, was concerned basically with the soul of mankind rather than with the souls of men, which called, by the very nature of its deep-seated disease, for a mighty cosmic cure on the part of God. Forsyth would have had little patience with our modern psychological 'confessionals,' with their underlying 'atomic' view of human personality. 'A remedy for such a situation which is merely simple is a pill for an earthquake, or a poultice for a cancer.'

So he directs us in his devotions to the Cross of Christ

25

—to God's deed upon the world soul; and the object of his 'minor'—albeit his most intimate writings—is not to lift a lame *psyche* over a stile but to offer in Christ's stead a way of healing to a sick and distressed world. In short, these books are really missionary tracts concerned with the dread plight of man's soul and God's travail to redeem it *on a world scale*.

The phrase 'practical writings' also needs defence. It suggests too readily that Forsyth was a speculative theologian of the 'balcony' type, who only on rare occasions came down from his isolated seat to deal with the issues of life. Nothing could be further from the truth. What John Newton wrote about his own theological schooling might be said of Forsyth's: 'My course of study, like that of the surgeon, has principally consisted in walking the hospital.' Like George Crabbe, who in the interests of literary realism visited the 'foulest ward,' Forsyth made a similar inspection in the cause of theological reality, not chiefly, however, to sound the misery of men, but to scan the heights and plumb the depths of the holy love of God. In this sense *all* his writings are practical. What has been said of Dale might be written of him: 'His theology was his own; won by the sweat of his own brain; the pain and beating of his own heart; interpreted by the experience of his own life.' His searching writing was not elaborated from books, or in seclusion from the interests of men, but it was hammered out on the anvil of life and society. It is significant that his earliest utterances are concerned with moral questions and the problems of men in society. Forsyth was one of our earliest modern writers on Christian sociology.

This Anthology is primarily concerned with those writings which were preached before they were written, and were addressed not to the theological student but to the people, dressed in the homespun of the people's tongue to meet the spiritual needs of Everyman.

These books—so small in compass—afford the very marrow of the Christian faith, and were the basis of the more academic and specialized works which Forsyth was to write later.

Forsyth himself said, 'You must live with people to know their problems, and live with God in order to solve them.' This divine-human polarity is seen almost on every page of these selections. One object of this book is to encourage the more detailed study of Dr Forsyth's writings in their complete form. We therefore draw the attention of the reader to the uniform editions of the more important of Forsyth's books published by the Independent Press. *The Person and Place of Jesus Christ*, *This Life and the Next*, *The Work of Christ*, *Positive Preaching and the Modern Mind*, *The Cruciality of the Cross*, *The Church and the Sacraments*, *The Charter of the Church*, and others, are now obtainable in an attractive format.

We wish to express our appreciation of the kindness of Mrs Jessie Forsyth Andrews in permitting quotation from some of these books, and to Independent Press for sponsoring the present one and including it in their galaxy of books by and about Dr Forsyth.

Anthology Part I

THE PLIGHT OF MAN

Life grows more and more severe. Pain becomes more inward—more in the nature of care, fear, or despair. It is, therefore, more intractable and taxing. . . . Grief and strain advance along with physical security and comfort. Civilization only internalizes the trouble. We have fewer wounds, but more weariness. We are better cared for, but we have more care.

—P.T.F.

The Cost of Liberty

ONCE I got a lesson and a rebuke. You remember the Wars of the Roses, the Red Rose, the House of Lancaster, and John of Gaunt? Well, I went to see Lancaster not long ago, and the great old castle, now a jail, where John lived. Lancaster commands a lovely view. You look across the silver stretch of Morecambe Bay, and your eye rests on the hills around the English Lakes. There is Black Combe, Coniston Old Man, Helvellyn, and far to the right is Ingleborough. It was early March when I was there. The snow lay upon the mountains, and they shone in the sun as if they were the great white throne, and the waters of the Bay were like the crystal sea, and over all was the living light. My heart went forth, and I began to pine for the sight of mightier snows in foreign lands. We were standing upon the castle roof, and the dungeons were beneath our feet, modern cells, and old, old dungeons built by the Romans deep in the ground with neither light nor heat, nor breath of air. Then I thought how dreadful is the beauty of nature, like the beauty of the tiger's skin. Here I am standing to gaze upon it on the summit of deep, old misery, among the relics of cruelty and wrong. What did those beautiful hills ever care for the poor prisoners that for centuries have come and gone, deep shut away from the light? How could I help remembering that I should not have been so free to enjoy the sight, but for the struggles and captivities of such men as some of those who had lived and died beneath my feet? I had the light of Liberty which is more than the glory of a thousand hills. Ah! there is a more glorious light than the beauty of the world, and it comes not

from the throne of Nature but from him who sits there-
on!

—*Pulpit Parables*

Humanity Great in its Misery

WE inherit greatness and breathe it. Earth and sky and
day and night; stars in the naked heavens, breathings
of wind, and the coming of spring; hill and plain,
rolling tracts, and river and sea; the mists on the long,
wet moor, and above it the black, baleful cloud; fleets
and camps, cities and realms; valour and power,
science, trade, churches, causes, arts, charities; the
fidelities of peace and the heroisms of war, the rhythm
of order and the stream of progress; the generations
that go under and the civilizations that survive; the
energies unseen, the vanished past, the forgotten and
the unforgettable brave; the majesty of the moral hero
and the splendour of the public saint; agonies, love,
and man's unconquerable mind—Oh, we have a great
world, great glories, great records, great prospects, and
great allies! We inherit greatness, and we inhabit
promise. . . .

But as our sun rises there is a rising cloud. In the
moving soul there is a frail seam, an old wound, a
tender sore. The stout human heart has a wearing ache
and a haunting fear. There is a hollow in the soul's
centre, in its last hold no fortress, and in its sanctuary no
abiding God. A vanity blights the glory of time, a
lameness falls on the strenuous wing, our sinew shrinks
at certain touches, and we halt on our thigh; pride
falters, and the high seems low, and the hour is short,

and the brief candle is out, and what is man that he is accounted of? There is a day of the Lord upon all that is haughty, on lofty tower, and tall cedar, and upon all pleasant imagery. And misery, sin, and death grow great as all our triumph dwindles on the sight. They baffle the wisdom of the wise, and they are stronger than the valour of the brave. The city heroes are feasted in the morning, and the city streets are a hell at night. And the heart's cheer fails, and love yields to death, and we cannot, cannot, bear it. Memory turns to terror—not only for lost love but lost purity. Conscience belittles all greatness, and submerges it all by the greatness of its law, evermore saying, Holy, holy, holy, is the Lord God of Hosts; and by the greatness of its cry, My wound, my wound! My grievous sin and my desolate end.

The greatness of the soul is more apparent in the greatness of its misery than in the triumph of its powers.

—The Taste of Death and the Life of Grace

The way to the soul's final greatness lies through its misery rather than through its success.

—The Taste of Death and the Life of Grace

Our Crises overwhelm our Christ

THE trouble of the time is this—that we are more universal in our thought and experience than we are in our faith. Our experience is wider than our faith. Death is wider than grace. Our ideas are wider than our real religion. Our culture is wider than our actual creed. Our crises overwhelm our Christ. Men range the world with ships, trains and wires. They range the universe

32

with microscope, telescope and spectrum. They explore human nature with the aid of genius, and they go far in that knowledge of the soul which comes of culture. History and geography, science and literature, serve us as they never did before. We are cosmopolitan, but are we really universal? We go far, but do we go deep? We have more experience than we have faith to carry. If masses are under-educated, masses are over-educated. Their resources submerge their conscience. And their conscience itself outruns their ethics. Men see a right which they cannot make a habit, or pass into public use. Their knowledge of the world is so great that it actually belittles their world. The more they know of it the less they think of it. Prosperity brings leanness of soul and meanness of ideal. The more they know of men the less they respect man. The more they see the less they believe. The more their experience the less their faith in the great faiths, hopes and gospels. They like broad views, often because these seem to make less demand on their bankrupt souls.

—*The Taste of Death and the Life of Grace*

Psychology or the Faith?

WE find ourselves after a delightful evening with the subliminal self, at deadly grips with a ferocious and ignoble passion. . . . How can we hope to regain the influence the pulpit has lost until we come with the surest Word in all the world to the guesses of science, the maxims of ethic, and the instincts of art?

—*Positive Preaching and the Modern Mind*

The Soul's Civil War

IT is not a world out of joint that makes our problem, but the shipwrecked soul in it. It is Hamlet, not his world, that is wrong. It is not the contradictions of life, and its anomalies, that make the real trouble, but the unfaith, the falsity of those who live. It is the soul's own civil war, the rebellion of man-soul, its sullen severance from God, its ostrich hope of escaping his law, its silly notions of making it up with him, its hate and dread of him, its sin, and the triviality of its sense of sin. *What we need is not new truth, new ideas, new theology.* What can any *truth*, new or old, do for sin? Sin is more than untruth, more than ignorance. What can ideas or theologies do for my wickedness? The truth about even God never convicted of sin. It was the coming of God. Christianity does not peddle ideas; it does things. Reality lies in action, and Christ has done the deed of history. *What we need is new power, new reality, and a new kind of it,* a regeneration not a reform, a holy, costly Saviour, and not a blessed saint. What we need most is neither to feel nor to act differently, but power to be different, to be a new creature, and live in a new world. And our world is not like America—just the other side of the old. It is another order of things, values, and powers in the Cross.

—*The Grace of the Gospel as the Moral Authority in the Church*

Philanthropy not Enough

IN some ways we are more in earnest with our age than with our Gospel for it. . . . Society is past saving by the philanthropists. It needs mighty evangelists. It is in our morals and not in our miseries that we confront the great realities of the world. It is an age's moral poverty that faces us, and something like the bankruptcy of the old spiritual house.

—The Grace of the Gospel as the Moral Authority in the Church

Anthology Part II

THE POWER OF GOD

It is the death of Christ that is the chief condition of modern progress. It is not civilization that keeps civilization safe and progressive. It is that power which was in Jesus Christ and culminated in his death and resurrection.

P.T.F.

I⊤ is not the preacher's prime duty then to find happy texts for the exposition of modern thought. Nor must he sink the Gospel to a revelation which puts people in a good humour with themselves by declaring to them that the great divine message is the irrepressible spirituality of human nature. It is an inversion of his work if he begin with Christ and enlarge into Goethe. Let him begin with Goethe, if he will, so that he go on to enlarge into Christ. Let him learn from the first part of Faust; he has nothing to learn from the second. Let him state the problem as powerfully as Shakespeare left it, but let him answer it with the final answer Christ left. No genius has or can have it but from Christ. For he is the answer that they but crave. And they but state, as only genius can, the human tragedy which it is Christ's to retrieve.

—Positive Preaching and the Modern Mind

The moral difficulty of society is not that we are strayed children, great babes in a wood. It is that we are sinful men in a sinful race. We are mutinous. It is not a pathetic situation that the preacher confronts so much as a tragic.

—Positive Preaching and the Modern Mind

A remedy for such a situation which is merely simple is a pill for an earthquake, or a poultice for a cancer.

—Positive Preaching and the Modern Mind

It is a much wickeder world than our good nature had come to imagine, or our prompt piety to fathom. We

38

see more of the world Christ saw. It calls for a vaster
salvation and a diviner Christ that we were sinking to
believe. And it must cast us back in resources in that
Saviour which the mental levity of comfortable religion,
lying back for a warm bath in its pew, was coming to
stigmatize as gratuitous theology.

—The Justification of God

Humanity needs the Theological Christ

THE non-theological christ is popular; he wins votes;
but he is not mighty; he does not win souls; he does not
break men into small pieces and create them anew.

—The Taste of Death and the Life of Grace

Man Cannot Atone

WE may sorrow and amend, but we cannot atone and
reconcile. Why, we cannot atone to each other, to our
own injured or neglected dead, for instance, our silent
inaccessible dead. I think of Carlyle's stricken widowhood. Neither by hand nor heart can we come at them,
nor bring them a whole lone life's amends. Our
jealous God monopolizes the right of atoning to them
for us. We cannot even beseech their forgiveness. We
cannot offer them ours. We cannot pray to them, we
can but pray *for* them. We can but pray to God to atone
to them for us. We may live, like Carlyle, to eighty in a
long, penitent widowhood, and *then* we cannot atone to
our wronged or lonely dead, nor smooth a feather of the
angels who tarried with us, and we never knew them

39

for angels till they had flown. . . . Nay, we cannot atone to our own souls for the wrong we have done them. We sin—and for us inexpiably—against our own souls. How much less, then, can we atone to our injured, neglected, sin-stung God. If our theology would let us, our conscience would not. The past cannot be erased, cannot be altered, cannot be repaired. There it stands. It can only be atoned; and never by us. If our repentance atoned, it would lose the humility which makes it worth most. It is atonement that makes repentance, not repentance that makes atonement.

—*The Holy Father and the Living Christ*

Revelation as Redemption

It is a miraculous vision that sees in that martyr more than a martyr—a Healer; and in the Healer more—the Redeemer. To see sin, sorrow, and death continually under the Cross, to see the grace of God triumphing over them in it, is the very soul and victory of faith. It is possible to see a beauty in sacrifice which draws the young imagination that way bent into a certain enthusiasm and imitation of the Cross. The high, but hollow, naturalism of George Eliot had room for the action on Maggie Tulliver of Thomas à Kempis. But that is a faith too aesthetic or too subjective for the stay and victory of the thorough-going soul over the last moral horrors of the world. In London, in one twenty-four hours, there is more, if we knew it, than a faith like that could bear. . . . There is much more in the Cross than such a darkling faith has fathomed. The infinite, ultimate love of God is there. The gift and grace of God for the whole world is there. It is not simply nor chiefly the love of Christ for his brethren that is in the Cross. That was indeed uppermost in Christ's life; but in his death that is not direct but indirect; and the primary thing is Christ's obedience to God, and his action, therefore, as the channel of God's redeeming love. It is the love of God for the godless, loveless, hating world that is there. And it is there, not simply expressed but effected, not exhibited but enforced and infused, not in manifestation merely, but in judgement and decision. . . . The prince of this world is already judged. He acts today as a power, indeed, but only as a doomed power. His sentence went out in the Cross. And he knows it. Humanity was rescued from him there. The crisis of man's spiritual destiny is there. The *opus operatum* of history is there. It is not simply revelation, but revelation as redemption. It does not show, it does.

—*The Taste of Death and the Life of Grace*

The Silence of the Redeemer and the Redemption

But the great crisis itself transpired in the secret place of the Most High; and the silence of the Gospels reflects the Saviour's own reserve. It is the stillness of a quiet, earnest, strong, retiring man. Yea, it is the silence of the unwordly and unseen, the shadow of the holiest, the gaze of the Cherubim, the hush of the great white throne, of holy wars in high places, of far-off spiritual things—slow, subtle, solemn, spiritual things. The silence of the first creation no man heard or saw. That silence is repeated in the second. It is the silence of the moving heavens, of the rising sun, of the Resurrection in the cool, dim dawn of the Church's faith and love, of all the mightest action of the Holy Ghost—yea, of his witness borne in your hearts in this hour when I speak these holy names and presume to call these awful powers. If ye call upon the Father, pass the time of your sojourning here in fear—in reverent and godly fear. For this holy Fatherhood is at its heart the consuming fire.

—The Holy Father and the Living Christ

Now the doers of these great deeds have little to say of them. They are not speechless, not meaningless, but silent men. Heroes are not their own heralds. The Redeemer was not his own apostle. He spoke most of his Father, much of himself as his Father's Son, little of his achievements, and of the pain and cost of them next to nothing at all.

The more the Gospel says to us, the more we are impressed with its silence. There is a form of the thirst for souls, of religious eagerness, of evangelical haste and pious impatience which is far too voluble and active to be impressive. It is more youthful than faithful, more ardent than sagacious, more energetic than inspired. It would express everything and at once in word or deed. They forget that the ardent lucid noon hides the solemn stars, and heaven's true majesty of night, no less than does the thickest cloud. Of this there is no sign in Christ. His institutions were not devised in the interest of the world's speedy evangelization. He could wait for the souls he redeemed as well as for the God he revealed. The waiting energy of the Church is just as faithful as its forward movements, and at certain times more needful. Faith has ever a holy indifference and a masterly negligence which rest on the infinitude of divine care and the completeness of Christ's work.

—The Holy Father and the Living Christ

The Loneliness of Christ

How should a man feel who was alive, alone, in a world of the dead? It is beyond imagination desolate. To be alone on the earth with none but the dead, go where you might! It would be dreary and appalling enough for most men to be frozen up with one or two companions only in the Arctic Circle. To be there alone in a world of monotonous thick-ribbed ice, in the darkness of a long night, in driving snow-storms—what could be more desolate and awful? One thing, perhaps; to know, while there, that you were the only living soul on the earth, that if you returned to warmer suns you would find everyone dead, that the whole earth was one vast cemetery in which you were the only man alive. That would be what Shelley calls 'desolation deified.' Your mind could not bear this strain; you would go mad in the awful dreariness of such death. The taste of it would kill you physically. Is this imagery more awful or less awful than what Christ felt? Was Christ's agony below imagination or above it, beyond it? Too trifling or too solemn for it? His solitude was that of *the Life* amidst the dead world. The more he was the life the more power he had to feel death.

—*The Taste of Death and the Life of Grace*

The Hidden Cost of Redemption

THAT artist who works with such consummate ease, swiftness, and grace, how did he come by it? By hours

43

and years of cost, in practice, in drudgery, slavery, self-mastery, self-sacrifice, by a life he would often describe as one of labour and sorrow more than joy. But the master's art keeps all that out of sight. The grace he offers you is not to be spoiled by the obtrusion of such cost.

The friend you receive, and think nothing in the house too good for him—do you let him know of that trouble with the cook, of those hours of wakeful contrivance by which you earn the means of spending your hospitality on him, of that weakness of body which you master every time you laugh with him, that heartache which you keep down while you make everything so pleasant for him?

So God does not mar his grace by always thrusting on us what it cost.

—The Holy Father and the Living Christ

There is no precious freedom that costs nothing. Without blood, without cost, no remission, no release, no finding of the self, no possessing of the soul, no self-possession, no ease, grace, royalty, or liberty in the soul's matter or style. Without cross no crown for the soul. It is equally true of God and man. ... Art conceals art. The art in forgiving, the utter grace of it, conceals the art of redeeming, the dread labour, sorrow, and secret of it.

—The Holy Father and the Living Christ

Light in a Dark Place

LET us work ourselves deeper into our faith, and think out its principles. Or let us trust ourselves more to

44

those who really do so. It is not easy work. It is easy to be plain and obvious, but not easy to be light in a dark place. The professors of the obvious are many and weariful, but the seers of the moral order are few. It is easy to yield to the religious impressionist, and I do not deny he has some ground for his existence; but he has none for monopoly, none for monarchy in the Church. It is not easy to grasp principles and go with them, as with torches, through the moral mist that surrounds us. It is not easy to track their action in a luminous path across life's moor. But then it is not easy to do anything worth much. And the Church has no business to be so fond of easy effects, so dazzled by rapid ones, or so facile in sympathy. No doubt her first business is to evangelize the world, and her second to consecrate those she has evangelized, and her third is to help and heal those ignorant and out of the way. But it is a fourth, if it be no part of the others, to become the moral guide of society, and translate her holy Gospel into large social ethics closely relevant to the time.

— *A Holy Church the Moral Guide of Society*

The Reticence of God in Forgiveness

YOU find poor human creatures who never can overlook your mistake without conveying to you that it is as much as they can do. They think no little of themselves for doing it. They take care that you shall never forget their magnanimity in doing it. They keep the cost of your forgiveness ever before you. And the result is that it is not forgiveness at all. How miserable a thing it is instead! How this spirit takes the charm from the

45

reconciliation! How it destroys the grace of it! How penurious the heart it betrays! How it shrivels the magnanimity it parades! How grudging, how ungodlike it is! How unfatherly! What an ungracious way of dealing with the graceless.

That is not God's way of forgiveness. His Fatherhood has the grand manner. It has not only distinction, but delicacy. He leaves us *to find out* in great measure what it cost—slowly, with the quickened heart of the forgiven, to find that out. Christ never told his disciples he was Messiah till it was borne in on them by contact with him. He never told them till, by the working of the actual Messiahship upon them, they found it out. Revelation came home to them as discovery. It burst from experience. So gracious is God with his revelation that he actually lets it come home to us as if we had discovered it. That is his fine manner—so to give as if we had found.

—The Holy Father and the Living Christ

The Religious Failure of a Prodigal

WHAT should you think of the forgiven son, who, as the pardoned years went on, never took his mercy seriously enough to give a thought to what he had brought on his father or God? If he never cared to go behind that free forgiveness which met him and feasted him without an upbraiding word; if he never sought to look deep into those eyes which had followed him, watched him, and spied him so far; if he was never moved by the amazing

46

welcome to put himself in the depths of his Father's place; if he took it all with a light heart, and told the world that in forgiveness he felt nothing but gladness; if he said that was all we know and all we need to know; if the swift forgiveness of God made it easy for him to forgive himself and just forget his past; if the generous, patient father never became for him the Holy Father; if he felt it was needless and fruitless to enter into the dread depths of sin with the altar candle of the Lord, or explore the miracle of the Father's grace—what should you think of him then?

Give him, of course, a year or two, if need be, to revel in this glad and sweet surprise. Give to his soul (if need be) a holy honeymoon. But if the years go on and he show no thirst to search those things which the angels desire to look into, but cannot (being unhuman and unredeemed); if he never seek to measure the latent meaning of it all for the Redeemer, and give no sign of being deepened in conscience as the fruit of being redeemed there; if there be no trace of his coming to himself in a sense still deeper than when he turned among the swine; if he go on with a mere readiness of religious emotion, and a levity of religious intelligence which cares not to measure his sin by the finer standards of the Father's spirit, or gauge the holy severity of the love he spurned; if he learn nothing of the Lord's controversy and his mortal moral strife; if he weigh nothing of the sin of the world in the scales of eternal redemption—if his career in grace were such as that, what should we think of him then? Should we not have reason to doubt whether he was not disappointing the Father again, if he was not falling from grace in another way, and this time in a religious way?

—*The Holy Father and the Living Christ*

The Heroism of Christ in His Death

IT was death by sickly candlelight in a little house in a
back street among miles of them. It was death made
cheap, death for the million.

—The Taste of Death and the Life of Grace

He parted with what men call 'soul', or fine insight, and
took the state of the commonest, dreariest man or
woman who has been robbed of everything—fortune,
faculty, and feeling—except faith.

—The Taste of Death and the Life of Grace

The Aggravation of the Gospel

SOME people think it is such a nice, sweet, easy thing to
have to do with Jesus. They read pretty stories about
the child Jesus, and the Christmas time, and the
invitation to little children, and they feel that it must be
a very happy thing to be a Christbearer, to carry this
sweet image about the world. They are fond of talking
about the gentleness of Jesus, and the beauty of his
ways, and the lightness of his yoke. And they carry
Christ, as it were, on their shoulders, as if that were the
last and greatest thing, instead of being carried by him.
But a day comes when it is hard to carry Christ; when
what seemed a child is suddenly felt to be a man, nay,
to make the demands of a God upon your strength. You
enter the Christian life lightly, brightly, in the flower of
your strength, and the bloom of your enthusiasm. But

you soon find when the storms come, that the burden of Christ is a very, very heavy one, a serious one, which calls all your most earnest manhood and womanhood into play. The simplicity of Christ taxes all the depths of your soul and all the muscles of your conscience and will.

You took up the simple, gentle Christ, and you found before long that you had pressing on you the burden, the sin of the world. How could you come through it all if he did not carry you far more really than you him?

—Pulpit Parables for Young Hearers

We very properly hear much of the Gospel as amelioration; but we ought to hear more of it as aggravation. It makes men worse on the way to make them better. At least, it carries home and brings out the evil that is in them. Its law enters that sin may be shown to be sin, and the soul be shut up unto mercy by being cornered into despair. And it is another phase of the same action in the Gospel when its ideals turn our achievements to dust, and put us out of all conceit with our actual state. Its promises make us more impatient of the slow payment we receive, and its hopes make us resent more keenly the small instalments that arrive. The Gospel has fixed in the race, even of its deniers, a deeper conviction of destined bliss, and, therefore, pain is felt to be more of an intrusion. It is more of an intrusion into the ideal order of things. More people than ever before feel their right to happiness and resent its destruction. There is more anger at pain, and at the order of things including it. The mind of Europe is a magnified Job. We are rent asunder by a progressive culture and an arrested ethic, by an imagination that grows faster than the practical conditions of realizing it. Reality seems several lives beyond intuition. We dream a dream of good, but the Agnostics will not let us identify it with the ultimate reality of God. And for want of God our practical progress limps and halts far in the wake of our great surmise. And of the moral energy that we do have so much is engrossed with healing or preventing pain, that it is withdrawn from the noble enduring of it, from the conversion and sanctification of wounds incurable.

—The Taste of Death and the Life of Grace

These shall last

THE old dear names in their new creation are the divinest still, and the nearest at our need. They are the holiest and most human too. Father, mother, wife, child, lover, and maid—that is the old story of which the world never grows weary. Of the tale of romance and of renunciation we do not weary. Two lovers whispering by an orchard wall, these weeping for their first-born dead or lost, these chilled and estranged for ever, or these at last grown grey and sleeping together at the foot of the hill—such things outlast in their interest for us all the centuries of human care and crime. They outlive our folly, noise, and sin, earth's triumphs, glories, failures, fevers, and frosts. But not only so. They are immortal also in God. They are hid with Christ in God. Eternity does not draw a sponge over the heart. Our great passions are laid up beneath the altar of the Father's passion to redeem. They are smoothed out there where all crooked things are made straight. For us with our faith in Christ's Holy Father, love is not what the pessimists make it—Nature duping the individual in the interests of the species. It belongs to the eternal.

—The Holy Father and the Living Christ

The Emigration of the Divine

THE height of omnipotence was the power to humble himself, to empty himself, to go out of himself and his own bliss. He leaves his native and eternal blessedness and settles in a foreign world. The eternal Father expatriates himself, and in his Son becomes a Pilgrim Father to found a new world. Some speak of the world as due to emanations of the Divine. I would speak rather, if I reverently might, of the emigration of the Divine, of his going forth in his person, and not of his sending forth his waves. Might I venture on the expression that it was by a Divine emigration and settlement in Christ and his Spirit that earth became a colony of him and the Church a missionary colony upon the face of the earth? The real idea in the heart of creation was not by almighty magic to make something out of nothing, but it was by moral miracle to make himself of no account, to become a child and an alien on the earth, to suffer and to die. The thousand, the million, the Infinite, becomes a little one; and that is the way in which the little one ever becomes a thousand.

—The Empire for Christ

The Contemporaneity of the Word

I READ the story of the father who beseeches Christ to heal his son. I hear the answer of the Lord, 'I will come down and heal him.' '*Him*!' That means me. The words are life to my distempered soul. I care little for them (when I need them most) as an historic incident of the long past, an element in the discussion of miracles. They do not serve their divinest purpose till they come to me as they came to that father. They come with a promise here and now. I see the heavens open, and the Redeemer at the right hand of God. I hear a great voice from heaven, and these words are the words of the Saviour himself to me, 'I will come down and heal him.' And upon them he rises from his eternal throne, he takes his way through a ready lane of angels, archangels, the high heavenly host, and the glorious fellowship of saints. They part at his coming, for they know where he would go. These congenial souls do not keep him, and these native scenes do not detain him. But on the wings of that word he moves from the midst of complete obedience, spiritual love, holy intelligence, ceaseless worship, and perfect praise. He is restless amid all that in search of me—me, sick, falling, lost, despicable, desperate. He comes, he finds, he heals me on the wings of these words. I do not ask the critics for assurance that the incident took place exactly as recorded. I will talk of that when I am healed.

—The Grace of the Gospel as the Moral Authority in the Church

Anthology Part III

THE PERFECTION OF FAITH

Learn to commit your soul and the building of it to One who can keep it and build it as you never can.

P.T.F.

YOUR faith . . . may be perfected when everything else is very crude and fragmentary. Your attainments even in grace may be very poor, but your faith may be perfect. You may utterly trust him who saves to the uttermost. You may perfectly trust your perfect Lord, and charge him with the responsibility both for your sin and your sanctification. The perfectness of their trust is the only perfect thing about some; but it gives them perfection which people envy who are far richer in attainment and repute. Perfect faith is possible to some who, with many excellences, have no other perfection whatever. There are imperfect human beings whom we perfectly trust and love. There are faulty wives and husbands, parents and children, lovers and friends, who perfectly trust and love each other. There is no faculty so universal as this of perfect trust. How common it is I do not say; but it is the most universal in its nature. It is possible to those who can do nothing else. The child can exercise it. You can win it from many who are the despair of any other means of culture. The savage can learn it toward his missionary and still more toward Christ, when he is too low in the scale to acquire much from civilization beyond its vices. The perfection of faith is the hope of a universal religion. It is the great faculty of manhood. It is the great beauty of manhood and womanhood. It is the divine thing in love. It is the soul of marriage, whether of man and woman, or of mankind to Christ. Faith is the marriage of God's perfection and man's. It is the union of the perfection which is absolute and eternal with the perfection which is relative and perfectly *grows*. It is the human ideal, the

54

supreme exercise of human faculty. It is an incessant demand on us, and it is an opportunity not for an elect but for all, not for a caste but for the soul.

—*Christian Perfection*

By Faith Alone

EXPERIENCE works up from nature to infer God's power and glory; from human love to infer a divine tenderness and fatherhood; from personal history to implications about Christ and God. And that is the method of a subjective, literary and humanist age like the present. But faith works downward from its grasp of God in Christ alone, from its absolute and eternal certainties, to actual life. And it works not merely with an inference but with an ought; not with implications but with compulsions; with demands absolute in order to be final and effective; not upon thought or truth, but on conduct. It does not induce from life what God must be, but it deduces from God what life must be. It does not predicate about God; it prophesies about man. The experimental religion of true faith is not based on experience, but on revelation and faith. It is realized by experience, it proceeds in experience; but it does not proceed from experience. . . . Faith is our relation not to what we possess but to what possesses us. Our faith is not in our experience, but in our Saviour.

—*Christian Perfection*

Culpa Felix

EVERY defect of ours is a motive for faith. To cease to feel defect is to cease to trust. To cease to feel the root of sin would be to have one motive the less to cast us on God for keeping. Every need is there in order to rouse the need for God. And we need God chiefly, not as a means to an end, not to satisfy earthly need, to keep the world going, to comfort us, or to help us to the higher moral levels. We do not need God chiefly as a means even to our own holiness. But we need God for himself. He himself is the end. We need chiefly communion with him; which is not confined to the perfectly holy but is open to all in faith, and possible along with cleaving sin. To treat a living person as an end, to seek him for himself, has but one meaning. It is to love him, to have our desire and energy rest in him, to have our personal finality in him. So it is that we need and seek God, not his help nor his gifts—even of sanctity, but himself. His great object with us is not our sinlessness but our communion. 'Give me thy heart.' He does not offer us communion to make us holy; he makes us holy for the sake of communion.

—Christian Perfection

Unconscious Holiness

THE holiest have ever been so because they dared not feel they were. Their sanctity grew unconsciously from their worship of his. All saw it but themselves. The eye

56

is the beauty of the face because it sees everything but itself, and if it betray self-consciousness the charm is dimmed. The height of sinlessness means the deepest sense of sin. If we ever came to any such stage as conscious sinlessness we should be placing ourselves alongside Christ, not at his feet. We should have 'life in ourselves,' with him but not through him, or through him only historically. We should pass out of faith into experience, or actual, personal possession like our common integrity. We should be self-sufficient. We should cease to live on a constant look to God in Christ, and repentance would cease. We should be near the fall that so often comes to the sinless. We should be in the moral peril of those who, feeling they have attained this sinlessness, are ready to call each impulse good and lawful, as born from the Spirit with which they are now possessed. Moral perceptions are confused. Evil is called good because it is deduced from the Spirit. 'Out of a state of holiness can come no sin. I may do what I am moved to do and it is not sin.'

—Christian Perfection

Do not tell people how they ought to feel toward Christ. That is useless. It is just what they ought that they cannot do. Preach a Christ that will make them feel as they ought. That is objective preaching. The tendency and fashion of the present moment is all in the direction of subjectivity. People welcome sermons of a more or less psychological kind, which go into the analysis of the soul or of society. They will listen gladly to sermons on character-building, for instance; and in the result they will get to think of nothing else but their own character. They will be the builders of their own character; which is a fatal thing. Learn to commit your soul and the building of it to One who can keep it and build it as you

57

never can. Attend then to Christ, the Holy Spirit, the Kingdom, and the Cause, and he will look after your soul.

—The Work of Christ

We shall never be real or holy by trying to be either, but only by trusting and loving the Most Holy and Real. The age's soul can only find its forwandered self by trust toward a God forgiving and saving it on the scale of all history in the hell-harrowing, heaven-scaling Cross of Christ.

—The Grace of the Gospel as the Moral Authority in the Church

True spirituality is not the highest stage of the blossoming world, but it is the world beaten, broken, and led captive. It stands not on the world's development, but on a break with the world, the inroad of a new life in a new kind.

—The Grace of the Gospel as the Moral Authority in the Church

The Real Moral Heroism

YOUR heroism is not in encountering the great temptations with the elation of strength, but in meeting the mean, incessant, wearing temptations through moral habit bred from past elations; when you have to drag yourself to the conflict, benumbed in vitality, and alive only in trained faith to the grace and goodness of a darkling God.

—The Taste of Death and the Life of Grace

58

Exploiting God

No inner process, no discipline to which we might subject ourselves, no way of cultivating subjective holiness would do so much for us as if we could lose ourselves, and in some godly sort forget ourselves, because we are so preoccupied with the mind of Christ. If you want psychological analysis, analyse the will, work, and purpose of Christ our Lord. I read a fine sentence the other day which puts in condensed form what I have often preached about as a symptom of the present age: 'Instead of placing themselves at the service of God most people want a God who is at their service.' These two tendencies represent in the end two different religions. The man who is exploiting God for the purposes of his own soul or for the race, has in the long run a different religion from the man who is putting his own soul and race absolutely at the disposal of the will of God in Jesus Christ.

—The Work of Christ

Wanted Twice-Born Men

WE want the new song of those who stand upon the rock, taken from the fearful pit and the miry clay, with the trembling still upon them and the slime still moist. We want the devotion of men whom grace found, and scarcely saved in the jaws of death, and took from the belly of hell. We want more joy, but more of the joy of

59

men who have tasted death either in their own conscience or in the communion of their Redeemer's. We
need it to make Faith what in some of its popular forms
it is ceasing in any imperial way to be—a power and a
passion in authority among the passions and powers of
the race.

—The Taste of Death and the Life of Grace

There is no persuasiveness like that of men who have
known the terror of the Lord. There is no reason so
authoritative as supernatural grace—amazing and
incomprehensible.

—The Taste of Death and the Life of Grace

There are men and women whose faith from their
early years is simple, ready, and sure. They are not the
victims of a deadly struggle. It is not theirs to clear a
path with spiritual agony from darkness into light, and
rise from despair into faith and hope. But that is the
heavy destiny of many another, who only comes to the
simplicity of trust in his later years, and only gains the
peace of confident love after he has been exercised and
strengthened by the searching conflict of many a
spiritual fight. Is that late-won faith just the same as the
early trust which seemed to come into life with the
temperament, as a natural endowment and personal
gift? Is the faith of the twice-born worth no more than
that of the once-born? Surely no. He who has fought his
way to light has a grasp and sinew denied to the other's
gentle trust, and a power to lift others to his side. He
knows the ground he has covered with armed vigilance
as the cheery traveller does not. He has a power of
sympathy with other serious wayfarers which is absent
in those to whom the burden was light. And to the
faith of the warrior a whole world of deep significance

and rich association lies open, where the more childlike mood feels but a vague spiritual presence and a dim sense of voiceless, balmy breath.

—Christct on Parnassus

Faith the Key to Holiness

Do not fret yourself examining your faith, trying its limbs, feeling its pulse, watching its colour, measuring its work. See rather that it is set on a living Christ. Care for that Christ and he will care for your faith. Realize a living Christ, and he will produce in you a living faith. Visit his holy sepulchre in Scripture, and as you pore and wait he will surprise you from behind with his immortal life.

—The Holy Father and the Living Christ

Responsibility Greater than Freedom

IT is useless to preach the kingdom when we do not carry into the centre of life the control of a King. The first duty of every soul is to find not its freedom but its Master. And the first charge of every church is to offer, nay to mediate, him.

—Positive Preaching and the Modern Mind

If within us we find nothing over us we succumb to what is around us.

—Positive Preaching and the Modern Mind

The first duty of a man is not to assert a freedom, nor to use a private judgement, but to find an absolute Master.

—Positive Preaching and the Modern Mind

As we become civilized we grow in power over everything but ourselves, we grow in everything but power to control our power over everything.

—The Justification of God

To lose Faith in Christ is to lose Faith in Man

IT is faith in Christ that has kept belief in a God from dying out in the world. It is never the arguments of the thinkers or the intuitions of the saints that have done that. If Christ grow distant and dim, the sense of a living personal God, of Christ's God and Father, fades from the soul, and the power of God decays from life. And what happens then? We lose faith in man—in each other, and in ourselves.

—The Holy Father and the Living Christ

Perfection is Wholeness

A MAN may abide in the many-mansioned, myriad-minded Christ, even if the robber sometimes break into his room, or if he go out and lose his way in a fog. You stay in a house, or in a town, which all the same you occasionally leave for good or for ill. The question is, What is your home to which your heart returns, either in repentance or in joy? Where is your heart? What is the bent of your will on the whole, the direction and service of your total life? It is not a question settled in a quantitive way by inquiry as to the occupation of every moment. God judges by totals, by unities not units, by wholes and souls, not sections. What is the dominant and advancing spirit of your life, the total allegiance of your person? Beethoven was not troubled when a performer struck a wrong note, but he was angry when he failed with the spirit and idea of the piece. So with the Great Judge and Artist of life. He is not a school-master, but a critic; and a critic of the great sort, who works by sympathy, insight, large ranges, and results on the whole. Perfection is not sinlessness, but the loyalty of the soul by faith to Christ when all is said and done. The final judgement is not whether we have at every moment stood, but whether having done all we stand—stand at the end, stand as a whole. Perfection is whole-ness. In our perfection there is a permanent element of repentance. The final symphony of praise has a deep bass of penitence. God may forgive us, but we do not forgive ourselves. It is always a Saviour, and not merely an Ideal, that we confess. Repentance belongs to our abiding in Christ, and so to any true holiness.

—*Christian Perfection*

The Greatest Influences in Life

THE greatest element in life is not what occupies most of its time, else sleep would stand high in the scale. Nor is it even what engrosses most of its thought, else money would be very high. It is what exerts intrinsically the

63

most power over life. The two or three hours of worship and preaching weekly has perhaps been the greatest single influence on English life. Half an hour of prayer, morning and evening, every day, may be a greater element in shaping our course than all our conduct and all our thought; for it guides them both. And a touch or a blow which falls on the heart in a moment may affect the whole of life in a way that no amount of business or of design can do. Conduct is not the main thing. . . . Look to the faith, and the conduct must come. True faith has all ideal conduct in its heart and, what is more, in its power.

—*Christian Perfection*

Christ in the Soul

A LIVING Christ who only ruled his kingdom in the unseen *by general laws* would be no sufficient Saviour. He must be personal to us. He must be *our* Saviour, in *our* situation, *our* needs, loves, shames, sins. He must not only live but mingle with *our* lives. He must charge himself with *our* souls. We believe in the Holy Ghost. We have in Christ as the Spirit the Sanctifier of our single lives, the Reader of *our* hearts, the Helper of our most private straits, the Inspirer of *our* most deep and sacred confessions. We must have one to wring from us '*My* Lord and *my* God'. We need not only the risen Christ but the returned Christ; not only the historic Christ, nor the heavenly; but the spiritual, the intimate, the Husband of the soul in its daily vigour, its daily conflict, its daily fear, its daily joy, its daily sorrow, its daily faith, hope, love. We need, O how we need a Lord and

Master, a Lover and King of our single, inmost, shameful, precious souls, the Giver and the Goal of our most personal salvation, a Conscience within our conscience, and a Heart amidst our heart and its ruins and its resurrection.

That is the Christ we need, and, thank God for his unspeakable gift, that is the Christ we have.

—The Holy Father and the Living Christ

To hang upon Christ, and to do no more than hang, is to be a drag on Christ and a strain on man. To see and know him is to enter and live in him, to walk, run, mount, by the communion of his life. The fall of many who once were Christ's is because they took no serious means with themselves to prosecute their life in him, but were dragged in his wake till they got tired of the strain. There are men today who once tasted Christ, but their serious will was not given to their Christian life but to their affairs. And so the world, having monopolized their *will*, submerged their soul. And to be dragged after Christ, submerged in a medium so dense as the world, means a friction and a strain so severe that they took their fatal relief by cutting the cord—and drifting.

—Christian Perfection

The Conclusion of the Whole Matter

To be perfect with God you must have Christ come *home*, come HOME, to you and sit by your central fire —come home to *you*, to YOU, as if for the moment mankind were centred in the burning point of your soul, and you touched the burning point of God's. You must court and haunt his presence till it break forth on you, and it become as impossible not to believe as to believe is hard now. Then we realize what we were made for, made to be redeemed; we lay hold by faith of our destiny of perfection in another; we are already in spirit what it is latent in redemption that we shall be—what some curse in our nature seemed before to forbid and thwart our being. Our dry rod blossoms. We put forth buds one after another along the line of life. We grow into a stately, seemly tree, whose boughs are for shelter and whose leaves are for healing. Our pinched hearts expand, our parched nature grows green. The fever of life is cooled. Its fret is soothed. Its powers stand to their feet. Its hopes live again. Its charities grow rich. We feel in that hour that this is what we were made for, and we are sure that we are greater than we know. We find ourselves. We lose our load. We are delivered from our plague. Our weakness is made strong. Our enemies flee before us. Our promised land is round us. Life beckons where it used to appal. And all things with us are returning, through Christ, to the perfection of God from whom they came.

—*Christian Perfection*

Anthology Part IV

THE SOUL OF PRAYER

I saw in a friend's house a photograph from (I think) Dürer—just two tense hands, palms together, and lifted in prayer. It was most eloquent, most subduing. I wish I could stamp the picture on the page here and fit it to Milton's line: 'The great two-handed engine at OUR door.'

P.T.F.

What is True Religion?

It is not the religion which contains most truth in the theological sense of the word. It is not the religion most truly thought out, nor that which most closely fits with thought. It is religion which comes to itself most powerfully in prayer. It is the religion in which the soul becomes very sure of God and itself in prayer. Prayer contains the very heart and height of truth, but especially in the Christian sense of truth—reality and action. In prayer the inmost truth of our personal being locks with the inmost reality of things, its energy finds a living Person acting as their unity and life, and we escape the illusions of sense, self, and the world. Prayer, indeed, is the great means of appropriating, out of the amalgam of illusion which means so much for our education, the pure gold of God as he wills, the Spirit as he works, and things as they are.

—The Soul of Prayer

The Peril of Mysticism

It is our tendency to think that the way to reach a warm and steady revelation of God is to go deep into the interior of human nature, away from those infinities and sanctities that approach it so coldly from without. And so we say, 'Sink into yourself and rise redeemed.' Pierce the human and you will find the divine. Penetrate far enough into the human heart and you reach the real presence of a loving God. Make the most of human affection and you arrive at the love of God. Open the heart of a divine man and you will find the heart of a human God. It is an error which I may illustrate by another. It is a popular notion that the warmest part of this island must be in the centre of it, away from the cold waters and high gales of the inconstant sea. But the scientific fact is just the reverse. The sea has a benign and steadying influence upon the climate of the coast. The coldest place in England, according to the charts, is a spot at its very heart. So it is not by retreating into the interior of our humanity or culture that we find the benign and blessed God. The bustle of passion and energy at our human centre can be spiritually colder than where men face the realities that close us in. At the heart of man you will find divine symptoms, but not a divine salvation. *Tendimus in altum*. There is a circumambient grace in the theologies despised by the humanities, a grace that comes to our shore and knocks, yea beats, and even lashes, there; and it has more of the changeless love of God in it than all the affections that sweeten the inlands of life, or the culture that adorns it. Sea and shore may indeed meet in storm. But our peace lies through storm. Our state is such that our salvation is where God and man meet in an historic crisis, where God's passion to reach us falls upon man's rock-bound will not to be found. Herein is love, not that we love, but that God loves and makes awful propitiation for us—

> *The best of all we are and do*
> *Just God forgive.*

—*The Grace of the Gospel as the Moral Authority in the Church*

On the voyage of the Church we need daily to 'take the sun.' Experience of the Gospel, moral, personal, daily, is the only fidelity to the Gospel, and its only guarantee against decadence.

—*The Grace of the Gospel as the Moral Authority in the Church*

The Bible and the Word

THE Word is not in the Bible as a treasure hid in a field so that you can dig out the jewel and leave the soil. It grows from it like a tree. It breathes from it like a sweet savour. It streams up from it like an exhalation. It rises like the soul going to glory from its sacred dust. The Word of God is not to be dissected from the Bible, but to be distilled.

—*The Grace of the Gospel as the Moral Authority in the Church*

Prayer an Art

IT is an art—this great and creative prayer—this intimate conversation with God. '*Magna ars est conversari cum Deo,*' says Thomas à Kempis. It has to be learned. In social life we learn that conversation is not mere talk. There is an art in it, if we are not to have a table of gabblers. How much more is it so in the conversation of heaven! We must learn that art by practice, and by keeping the best society in that kind. Associate much with the great masters in this kind; especially with the Bible; and chiefly with Christ. Cultivate his Holy Spirit. He is the grand master of God's art and mystery in communing with man. And there is no other teacher, at last, of man's art of communion with God.

—*The Soul of Prayer*

The Bible and Prayer

PRAYER is for the religious life what original research is for science—by it we get direct contact with reality. The soul is brought into union with its own vaster nature— God. Therefore, also, we must use the Bible as an original; for, indeed, the Bible is the most copious spring of prayer, and of power, and of range. If we learn to pray from the Bible, and avoid a mere cento of its phrases, we shall cultivate in our prayer the large humane note of a universal gospel. Let us nurse our prayer on our *study* of our Bible; and let us, therefore, not be too afraid of *theological* prayer. True Christian prayer must have theology in it; no less than true theology must have prayer in it and must be capable of being prayed. . . .

Prayer and theology must interpenetrate to keep each other great, and wide, and mighty. The failure of the habit of prayer is at the root of much of our light distaste for theology.

—*The Soul of Prayer*

OUR Prayer Book, the Bible, does not prescribe prayer, but it does more—it inspires it. And prayer in Christ's name is prayer inspired by his first interest—the Gospel. Do not use Christ simply to countersign your egoist petition by a closing formula, but to create, inspire, and glorify it.

—*The Soul of Prayer*

Incessant Prayer

EVERY man's life is in some sense a continual state of prayer. For what is his life's prayer, but its ruling passion? All energies, ambitions, and passions are but expressions of a standing *nisus* in life, of a hunger, a draft, a practical demand upon the future, upon the unattained and the unseen. Every life is a draft upon the unseen. If you are not praying toward God you are toward something else. You pray as your face is set— toward Jerusalem or Babylon. The very egotism of craving life is prayer. The great difference is the object of it. To whom, for what, do we pray? The man whose passion is habitually set upon pleasure, knowledge, wealth, honour, or power is in a state of prayer to these things or for them. He prays without ceasing. These are his real gods, on whom he waits day and night. He may from time to time go on his knees in church, and use words of Christian address and petition. He may even feel a momentary unction in so doing. But it is a flicker; the other devotion is his steady flame. His real God is the ruling passion and steady pursuit of his life taken as a whole. He certainly does not pray in the name of Christ. And what he worships in spirit and in truth is another God than he addresses at religious times. He prays to an unknown God for a selfish boon. Still, in a sense, he prays. The set and drift of his nature prays. It is the prayer of instinct, not of faith. It is prayer that needs total conversion. But he cannot stop praying either to God or to God's rival—to self, society, world, flesh, or even devil. Every life that is not totally inert is praying either to God or God's adversary.

—The Soul of Prayer

72

Humility in Prayer

WE are not humble in God's sight, partly because in our prayer there is a point at which we cease to pray, where we do not turn everything out into God's light. It is because there is a chamber or two in our souls where we do not enter in and take God with us. We hurry him by that door as we take him along the corridors of our life to see our tidy places or our public rooms. We ask from our prayers too exclusively comfort, strength, enjoyment, or tenderness and graciousness, and not often enough humiliation and its fine strength. We want beautiful prayers, touching prayers, simple prayers, thoughtful prayers, prayers with a quaver or a tear in them, or prayers with delicacy and dignity in them. But searching prayer, humbling prayer, which is the prayer of the conscience, and not merely of the heart or taste; prayer which is bent on reality, and to win the new joy goes through new misery if need be—are such prayers as welcome and common as they should be? Too much of our prayer is apt to leave us with the self-complacency of the sympathetically incorrigible, of the benevolent and irremediable, of the breezy octogenarian, all of whose yesterdays look backward with a cheery and exasperating smile.

—The Soul of Prayer

Make Prayer a Duty

SOMETIMES, again, you say, 'I will not go to church. I do not feel that way!' That is where the habit of an ordered religious life comes in aid. Religion is the last region for chance desires. Do it as a duty and it may open out as a blessing. Omit it and you may miss the one thing that would have made an eternal difference. You stroll instead, and return with nothing but an appetite—when you might have come back with an inspiration. Compel yourself to meet your God as you would meet your promises, your obligations, your fellow-men.

—The Soul of Prayer

Be Yourself at Prayer

Go into your chamber, shut the door, and cultivate the habit of praying audibly. Write prayers and burn them. Formulate your soul. Pay no attention to literary form, only to spiritual reality. Read a passage of Scripture and then sit down and turn it into a prayer, written or spoken. Learn to be particular, specific, and detailed in your prayer so long as you are not trivial. General prayers, literary prayers, and stately phrases are, for private prayer, traps and sops to the soul. To formulate your soul is one valuable means to escape formalizing it. This is the best, the wholesome, kind of self-examination. Speaking with God discovers us safely to ourselves. We *find* ourselves, come to ourselves, in the

Spirit. Face your special weaknesses and sins before God. Force yourself to say to God exactly where you are wrong. When anything goes wrong, do not ask to have it set right, without asking in prayer what it was in you that made it go wrong. It is somewhat fruitless to ask for a general grace to help specific flaws, sins, trials, and griefs. Let prayer be concrete, actual, a direct product of life's real experiences. Pray as your actual self, not as some fancied saint. Let it be closely relevant to your real situation. Pray without ceasing in this sense. Pray without a break between your prayer and your life. Pray so that there is a real continuity between your prayer and your whole actual life.

—The Soul of Prayer

Prayer as Self-Examination

PRAYER, true prayer, does not allow us to deceive ourselves. It relaxes the tension of our self-inflation. It produces a clearness of spiritual vision. Searching with a judgement that begins at the house of God, it ceases not to explore with his light our own soul. If the Lord is our health he may need to act on many men, or many moods, as a lowering medicine. At his coming our self-confidence is shaken. Our robust confidence, even in grace, is destroyed. The pillars of our house tremble, as if they were ivy-covered in a searching wind. Our lusty faith is refined, by what may be a painful process, into a subtler and more penetrating kind; and its outward effect is for the time impaired, though in the end it is increased. The effect of the prayer which admits God into the recesses of the soul is to destroy that spiritual

75

density, not to say stupidity, which made our religion cheery or vigorous because it knew no better, and which was the condition of getting many obvious things done, and producing palpable effect on the order of the day. There are fervent prayers which, by making people feel good, may do no more than foster the delusion that natural vigour or robust religion, when flushed enough, can do the work of the kingdom of God. There is a certain egoist self-confidence which is increased by the more elementary forms of religion, which upholds us in much of our contact with men, and which even secures us an influence with them. But the influence is one of impression rather than permeation, it overbears rather than converts, and it inflames rather than inspires. This is a force which true and close prayer is very apt to undermine, because it saps our self-deception and its Pharisaism.

—The Soul of Prayer

Prayer Carries with it a Vow

A PRAYER is also a promise. Every true prayer carries with it a vow. If it do not, it is not in earnest. It is not of a piece with life. Can we pray in earnest if we do not in the act commit ourselves to do our best to bring about the answer?

—The Soul of Prayer

The Sin of Prayerlessness

NOT to want to pray . . . is the sin behind sin. And it ends in not being able to pray. That is its punishment—spiritual dumbness, or at least aphasia, and starvation. We do not take our spiritual food, and so we falter, dwindle, and die. 'In the sweat of your brow ye shall eat your bread.' That has been said to be true both of physical and spiritual labour. It is true both of the life of bread and of the bread of life.

—*The Soul of Prayer*

Prayer as Obedience

WE can offer God nothing so great and effective as our obedient acceptance of the mind and purpose and work of Christ. It is not easy. It is harder than any idealism. But then it is very mighty. And it is a power that grows by exercise. At first it groans, at last it glides. And it comes to this, that, as there are thoughts that seem to think themselves in us, so there are prayers that pray themselves in us. And, as those are the best thoughts, these are the best prayers. For it is the Christ at prayer who lives in us, and we are conduits of the Eternal Intercession.

—*The Soul of Prayer*

Criticism of Prayer dissolves in the Experience of it

Do not allow your practice in prayer to be arrested by scientific or philosophic considerations as to *how* answer is possible. That is a valuable subject for discussion, but it is not entitled to control our practice. Faith is at least as essential to the soul as science, and it has a foundation more independent. And prayer is not only a necessity of faith, it is faith itself in action.

Criticism of prayer dissolves in the experience of it. When the soul is at close quarters with God it becomes enlarged enough to hold together in harmony things that oppose, and to have room for harmonious contraries. For instance: God, of course, is always working for his Will and Kingdom. But man is bound to pray for its coming, while it is coming all the time. Christ laid stress on prayer as a necessary means of bringing the Kingdom to pass. And it cannot come without our praying. Why? Because its coming is the prayerful frame of soul.

—The Soul of Prayer

Science and Prayer

If I must choose between Christ, who bids me pray for everything, and the savant, who tells me certain answers are physically and rationally impossible, must I not choose Christ? Because, while the savant knows much about nature and its action (and much more

78

than Christ did), Christ knew everything about the God of nature and his reality. He knew more of what is possible to God than anybody has ever known about what is possible in nature.

—*The Soul of Prayer*

Prayer and Social Reconstruction

IT is the great producer of sympathy. Trusting the God of Christ, and transacting with him, we come into tune with men. Our egoism retires before the coming of God, and into the clearance there comes with our Father our brother. . . . When God fills our heart he makes more room for man than the humanist heart can find.

—*The Soul of Prayer*

Prayer is a greater school and discipline of divine love than the service of man is.

—*The Soul of Prayer*

Prayer alone prevents our receiving God's grace in vain. Which means that it establishes the soul of a man or a people, creates the moral personality day by day, spreads outward the new heart through society, and goes to make a new ethos in mankind.

—*The Soul of Prayer*

It settles at last whether morality or machinery is to rule the world.

—*The Soul of Prayer*

THERE is no such engine for the growth and command of the moral soul, single or social, as prayer. Here, above all, he who will do shall know. It is the great organ of Christian knowledge and growth. It plants us at the very centre of our own personality, which gives the soul the true perspective of itself; it sets us also at the very centre of the world in God, which gives us the true hierarchy of things. Nothing, therefore, develops such 'inwardness' and yet such self-knowledge and self-control. Private prayer, when it is made a serious business, when it is formed prayer, when we pray audibly in our chamber, or when we write our prayers, guided always by the day's record, the passion of piety, and above all the truths of Scripture—is worth more for our true and grave and individual spirituality than gatherings of greater unction may be. Bible searching and searching prayer go hand in hand. What we receive from God in the Book's message we return to him with interest in prayer. Nothing puts us in living contact with God but prayer, however facile our mere religion may be. And therefore nothing does so much for our originality, so much to make us our own true selves, to stir up all that it is in us to be, and hallow all we are. In life it is not 'dogged that does it' in the last resort, and it is not hard work; it is faculty, insight, gift, talent, genius. And what genius does in the natural world prayer does in the spiritual. Nothing can give us so much power and vision. It opens a fountain perpetual and luminous at the centre of our personality, where we are sustained because we are created anew and not simply refreshed. For here the springs of *life* continually rise. And here also the eye discerns a new world because it has second sight. It sees two worlds at once. . . . Here we learn to read the work of Christ which commands the world unseen. And we learn to read even the strategy of Providence in the affairs of the world. To pray to the Doer must help us to understand what is done. Prayer, as our greatest work, breeds in us the *flair* for the greatest work of God, the instinct of his kingdom, and the sense of his track in time.

—The Soul of Prayer

Prayer is the assimilation of a holy God's moral strength.

—The Soul of Prayer

Prayer alone prevents our receiving God's grace in vain. Which means that it establishes the soul of a man or a people, creates the moral personality day by day, spreads outward the new heart through society, and goes to make a new ethos in mankind. We come out with a courage and a humanity we had not when we went in, even though our old earth remove, and our familiar hills are cast into the depths of the sea. The true Church is thus co-extensive with the community of true prayer.

—The Soul of Prayer

The Eternal Intercessor

THE Redeemer would be less than eternal if he were not Intercessor. The living Christ could not live and not redeem, not intercede. Redemption would be a mere act in time if it were not prolonged as the native and congenial energy of the Redeemer's soul in the Intercession of Eternity.

—The Holy Father and the Living Christ

Do not picture Christ the Intercessor as a kneeling figure beseeching God for us. It is God within God; God in self-communion; God's soliloquy on our behalf; his word to himself, which is his deed for us.

—The Holy Father and the Living Christ

The intercession of Christ is simply the prolonged energy of his redeeming work. The soul of Atonement is prayer. The standing relation of Christ to God is prayer. The perpetual energy of his Spirit is prayer. It is prayer (and *his* prayer) that releases for us the opportunities and the powers of the spiritual world. It is the intercession of Christ that is the moving force within all the spiritual evolution of history. It is the risen Redeemer that has the keys of the world unseen—the keys which admit it to history as well as open it to man. The key of the unseen is prayer. That is the energy of the will which opens both the soul to the Kindom and the Kingdom to the soul. But never *our* prayer. It is prayer *for* us, not *by* us.

—The Holy Father and the Living Christ

Anthology Part V

THE CRISIS OF DEATH

Death is less regarded with supernatural awe. Men think of it more as a form of pain than as a spiritual experience.

P.T.F.

The Ministry of Death

WE might grant that death teaches us much as to the value of life, and that life without death would become a very hard and coarse thing. With the abolition of death would vanish the uncertainty which educates faith, the mystery, the tragedy, which makes life so great, the sense of another world which gives such dignity and meaning to this, the range of sympathy that flows from believing that our affections are not for this world alone. Erase death, and Tithonus tells us life sinks at last into drab weariness. Its noblest, dearest interest ebbs and fades. Its tragedy and its chivalry both go. We should end by having no concern but feeding, drowsing, prancing, and feeding again. Love, valour, pity, sacrifice; charm, music, and all the nameless spell of nature and of personality; courtesy and reverence, all the sweet fine things of life that are tributes to soul, and that death seems to cut short most painfully—those are the things which would really die out if we succeeded in indefinitely averting death.

—This Life and the Next

The Pity of God

THE ruling passion of the infinite God toward the little one surely must be pity. You have that patient process illustrated in the growth of man from the infant. All the most excellent faculty of the greatest man was once in the puling fashion of a helpless child. To his

84

mother, he was not great at all, but only dear. The mightiest monarch or genius or saint could once do no more for himself than the beggar's baby, and when they were stripped and washed you could not tell the one from the other. Naked we every one came into the world—naked of all those distinctions which grow upon life, and turn its first simplicity into so complex a thing. Naked, helpless, pitiable, the baby man appears, needing all manner of care, more care than the young of any other creature, and for a longer time. He appeals to pity and affection, and without them he must die. He moves the pity and love of women, and his true guardian angel is his mother. And if it be a long time since any of us said 'mother,' in heaven our angel doth always behold the face of our Father in heaven. But the poor little one moves more than a mother's pity when it is plunged so utterly helpless into such an old and clever world, he has the pity of God. Like a father the Lord pitieth these feeble things, bewildered and stunned at their entry on such a cunning world as this.

May we not let fancy go? May we not figure the helplessness and speechlessness of the babe as due to its utter bewilderment with the shock of emerging, naked and alone, upon such an awful stage, and a house so full and fine? But there falls upon the child, like a sheltering cloud, the pity of God. That is also unspeakable, like the amazement of its own wild, unspeculative eyes. And so these two look at each other and say nothing. The pity of the Lord shelters the child in a cloud of ignorance, and that pity is the first and closest swaddling clothes the infant wears.

And it is the pity of the Lord that rears it by all the sweet nursing mothers and all the strong nursing fathers, and all the stern and helpful shocks of life; it is still the pity of the Lord that makes a world for the soul to unfold in, and it is the faithful merciful Creator who adds the cubits to its stature and the faculty to its will. By the Lord's pity and grace the little one becomes a thousand, and the poor thing a great hero, and the manger-born a mighty saviour. May I not go farther, may I not whisper this? At last all the kingly faculty of man falls upon its second childhood; he re-enters the manger in the shape of a coffin. He has to accept the humiliation and the new birth of death; he has again to enter a vast strange world. Do you not think, when he emerges into that unseen world, and into the awful wonder, wisdom, and glory there, he will feel alone, bewildered, and stunned again as when he was born here? The old man is but an infant of days as he enters that world in which this world is but as a womb. And can you not believe that there God, the faithful Creator, awaits him, the measureless infinite pity of the Lord will be beforehand with the poor soul, and will prepare a place and take him up in his arms and call a nurse who (like Moses') may be his mother, or his Beatrice, like Dante's, and slowly that Grace will open his second life to the Love that moves the sun and all the stars.

And our immortality, like our mortality, will thus begin in the same Lord's merciful care which has borne us and carried us all the days of old.

—The Empire for Christ

Our Blessed Dead

THERE are those who can quietly say, as their faith follows their love into the unseen, 'I know that land. Some of my people live there. Some have gone abroad

86

there on secret foreign service, which does not admit of communications. But I meet from time to time the Commanding Officer. And when I mention them to him he assures me all is well.'

—This Life and the Next

Prayer for the dead is healthier than tampering with them. . . . In Christ we cannot be cut off from our dead nor they from us wherever they be. And the contact is in prayer.

—This Life and the Next

Anthology Part VI

ETERNAL LIFE

It is much to live for Eternity, to live Eternity is more.

P.T.F.

The Christian Ground for Immortality

A SURE belief in immortality does not rest where philosophy puts it, but where religion puts it. It is not founded on the nature of the psychic organism, but on its relation to Another. I mean that if it is based on the indestructible nature of the soul substance, or upon an untamed passion for adventure, or upon endless curiosity, or upon our instinct and thirst for personal perfection, or upon our native moral greatness, or upon any such stoic forms of self-esteem, or even self-respect, it is quite likely . . . to end downward in a supreme care for *my* immortality, whatever becomes of yours. And that ends in people elbowing each other out of the way to get at the elixir of life, or to dip in this Bethesda pool for Eternity.

—This Life and the Next

If my immortality is due to God's gift, it is due to his *incessant* gift and creation, and not to an infinite lease of life which he signed at the beginning. That is to say, it can go on only by communion with him.

—This Life and the Next

What man tends to say . . . is, 'Because I live I shall live'. But what Christ says, and what faith hears is, 'Because I live ye shall live also'. He alone has life in himself, and we have it by his gift and by union with him either here or hereafter.

—This Life and the Next

The Christian ground for immortality is that the Lord hath need of him.

—This Life and the Next

The Practice of Eternity

WE cannot tarry to argue if there is an immortality awaiting us; we must obey the immortality urging and lifting us. We do not move to a possible mirage of a City of God; the citizenship is within us. Ask, Am I living as immortal—not as one who will be immortal?

—This Life and the Next

Immortality is really a destiny pressing on us by Christ in us; it is not a riddle that just interests us. It is not chess; it is war. It is a duty bearing on us; it is not a theme that attracts us. When duties turn to mere problems and destinies become but intellectual toys, it is an evil time. It is not well when we stop doing in order to discuss.

—This Life and the Next

If you do not believe in it you cannot live it. And if you are not living an immortal life you are living something different and inferior; and the effect of this for life's tone and value must correspond. It is not something that begins when we die, but something that begins with us and lives forth in our life. Death is not the solution of the riddle, but a crisis of the power. And it may be the coming home of judgement on you for treating as a riddle what is a power.

—This Life and the Next

It is not the poverty and brevity of life that draws out its resources; it is its sense of fullness and power.

—This Life and the Next

91

I

WE are all predestined in love to life sooner or later, *if we will.*

—This Life and the Next

We threw away too much when we threw Purgatory clean out of doors. We threw out the baby with the dirty water of its bath. There are more conversions on the other side than on this, if the crisis of death opens the eyes as I have said.

—This Life and the Next

The dread of hell is an obsession that has distorted many lives. But that again has been because their future was more to them than Christ was, and they were more tied to self than freed in a Saviour. With a keen conscience and a vivid imagination, a future that is merely life prolonged and not reborn may well become filled with fears and loaded with care. But in Christ the future is given us filled with regenerate power and glory, where fear is sanctified into penitence and vigilance, sorrow glorifies God and becomes service, and love is realized in ready obedience. . . . Without Christ and the love of him, the past and the future may equally loom upon us, and beetle over our present.

—This Life and the Next

Man's true self is the worship of God's.

—This Life and the Next

Anthology Part VII

VIRGINIBUS PUERISQUE

Almighty Father, who knowest our downsitting and our uprising and art acquainted with all our ways, make us ever to be glad and rejoice before thee.

Give us the tractable spirit of hope and love and of a sound mind. Take away from us all ungodly fear and all inhuman hate, all fretful temper and all dark self-will.

Clothe our childhood with modest mirth and our age with beauty of holiness. May our life begin, continue, and end with thee.

Help us to take Jesus for our close companion and make men and women out of us in him. Make us thy blessed texts and write us like verses in thy great Book of Life, for ever and ever.

P.T.F.

The Man who lost his Shadow

I READ not long ago a famous story about a man who lost his shadow. It was told how he sold it away to a grey old man for a purse of gold which would never get low, take out of it what you would. Well, shadows seem very light, so at first the man never felt the want of his, and he liked to feel the heavy purse of gold, from which he filled chests and chests of treasure. But people began to notice his peculiarity. They talked of the rich man that had no shadow. They began to suspect him. The children from school ran after him; the old men pointed at him; then they got to fearing him. People conversing with him would notice all at once he had no shadow and would move hurriedly away. He was shunned and boycotted. Life became a misery to him because he was not as others are. He dared not venture out till the sun was gone down, and he had to rush home whenever the moon rose. He was a perfect burden to himself. He wandered and travelled without rest or end. He fell in love, and was just going to be married when the sad discovery was made, and it was all broken off. Misery rose wherever he went, but chiefly in his own heart. . . .

This poor man tried every way to get back his shadow. He found the grey old man who bought it, and he offered him his purse and all his gold back again if he would return the shadow. This the old man would not do, but he took the shadow out of his pocket, unfolded it, and made it dance before its true owner to torment him. Then he told him he could get his shadow back in only one way, namely, by selling his soul. 'Promise me', said the old rascal, 'that I shall have your soul when you die, and I will give you back your shadow.' Now you know, perhaps, who the old rogue was. But the poor shadowless man would not do that. So he wandered a vagabond over all the world, shunning men and shunned by them. He cursed his gold; and one day he threw the purse in disgust and anger down a deep pit. He could have no intercourse with his fellows but sought the study of nature—plants, and stones, and animals. He got a pair of seven-league boots and rambled easily over the earth, making wonderful scientific collections on his way, and, for all I know, he may be rambling about the world still, gaining, with sorrow, deep stores of knowledge, but ever unable to win the love or the trust of men.

Perhaps some lad who took a prize in elementary botany thinks he is not such a fool as to believe or care for a tale so silly as that. 'How could a man lose his shadow? Why should a man wish to lose it? And if he did, it wouldn't make all that difference. Why, they would put a person like that in a show nowadays, and make hatfuls of money by exhibiting him around the country. And he could live happy enough.' O! very good, my sharp little botany boy, but I fear you are much too clever ever to be very wise. Perhaps if you had been a black slave trying to escape in a town of white folks you would have been glad to part with that shadow upon your complexion. . . . The sharp botany boy and and the too-clever-by-half chemistry boy must stand down while I speak to the wiser children who love the wonders of a fairy tale. . . .

What does the shadow mean which the man parted with for gold? Well, I think it means trouble and sorrow; such trouble as every human heart is sure to meet with if it is a *loving* heart at all. And what we may learn is this, that if we set our hearts upon nothing else but escaping trouble, we shall only succeed in piling up

trouble of a far worse and more hopeless kind. . . .
Those who are always trying to escape all pain, and
who think of nothing but comfort, are sure one day to
get into trouble for which there is almost no remedy. If
you say in the winter, 'It is too cold, I can't go out, and
I don't want any exercise,' you will get so ill and so
restless that no exercise will do you any good, and you
will make a hard job for the doctor. And if you say, 'I
will keep my heart shut up, and I will love nobody, for
those I love may be ruined, or get ill, or die, and that
would make me suffer;' if you say that, and grow
selfish, and lay yourself out to make money and nothing
more, so that you may keep clear of all life's troubles and
share none of them with others, I bid you take warning
from the fate of the shadowless man. He parted with his
shadow for gold. He thought plenty of that would make
him happy, by ridding him of the dark and haunting
side of life. But sorrow is the shadow of joy, and you
can't have the one without the other. The heart that
feels no sorrow is a heart that feels no love. . . .

One day the shadows will of themselves flee away.
Where is it that there are no shadows? Near the
Equator. Why? Because the sun is straight over your
head. Your shadow is then exactly under your feet. So,
one day, when we stand far closer than we now are
under the presence and light of God, the shadow of
earth's trouble shall vanish. It will not be lost or
stolen, but it will be trodden under our feet. We shall
have conquered it in the light of the Lord. We shall
stand upon it, and it will neither haunt our way, nor
darken our past, nor cloud our future any more, for
ever and ever.

—Pulpit Parables for Young Hearers

A Seaside Sermon

I WAS born by the sea. I was brought up by the sea. A mile or two inland, in the dead of night, when all else was quiet, I used to hear the sea singing a lullaby to the fisher children on the shore beneath the moon and all her family of stars. Some people call the great world God's cathedral. Well, one of its organs is the sea. It can play as sweet and soft as a flute. But it can also roar and thunder to terrify the bravest. It is awful to hear the sea rolling in like mountains upon a shore of rocks and caves, and rousing echoes that are heard far inland as if many giants were roaring into many tuns. I suppose it is very silent at the bottom of the sea. The fishes and the shells may know nothing of all the concert amid which they live. But we can hear it, though we can hardly tell the words it sings. We can hear its music, so strange, mysterious, magical, and mighty. There are some hearts it can speak to, and they know what it says. They listen and they are soothed; or they listen and they feel something of rapture; or as they listen they feel something like terror; but always they love as they listen to the many sounds and the one great voice.

For the sounds are many that make the music of the sea. It may seem to you one great sound, but it is made up of many. As you lie by the sea on a breezy day you see the little white waves out there like sheep in a green field, or like cloudlets in the blue sky. Each one of them is making a little whisper as it runs along and breaks; and the sum of all their whispers must be something considerable, like the singing of a forest of little birds. Then there is the sound of every wave that tumbles on the shingle or the sand. Then there is the rush of it as it

97

runs along the beach. Then there is the hiss of it as it draws back. And there is the rattle of the pebbles one upon another which it carries back with it. Then there is the little clash as it meets another upcoming wave, and the pebbles are driven up again. Then there must be the sound of the tidal wave as it rises for hours and then sinks for hours away. Then streams are flowing with their own sound into the sea, or falling over cliffs with a trickle, or a splash, or a thud. Then children are paddling and splashing on the sand, and bathers are shouting and calling to each other. And you can hear the thump, thump of the steamer a mile off, and you can catch the creaking of the oars in that rowboat. And the ship yonder with all her sail set is hissing through the water, while her cordage creaks, and her mate shouts to the wheel, and the cabin boy is squabbling with the captain's dog. And the winds are piping in many keys, and the sea-birds are shrieking with wild, swift joy. And all these things are many sounds, which, perhaps, you do not separately hear, but they make up the one mysterious voice and music of the sea—a voice as rich and a music unfathomable as the great ocean deeps themselves. . . . We speak of the silent sea, but there is little silence there for those who have ears to hear. We speak of the silence of the hills too, but I could paint you a like picture of the hills, with the plash of water, the chirp of insects, the hum of bees, and the fluting of the winds, which would make you feel that these quiet hills are no more silent than the sea. The quiet things are sometimes the things that say most of all. And from silent people we can often learn more than from people who are always talking and always heard. You may be quite sure a quiet, brave man says more, and teaches us more, and delights us with the music of his modest courage more, than a man who is always boasting of what he has done or can do. The voice of the hills is the sound of many sounds, and the voice of the sea is the sound of many waters.

The little bit of sea that you look out on from your shore is a very small portion of the great ocean that encircles the world. And the sounds you hear are a very small part of the great voice which the many waters of the sea everywhere are sending up for music to the ear of Heaven. If you sat on a hill-top over a little town, you could hear something musical even in the shoutings of a mob, or the clamour of a market below. And so, if you sat at the right hand of God, who has all the world at his feet, what unspeakable music would rise to your ears from the manifold and awful concert of the mighty sea! Voices would come from east, west, north, and south, from pole and equator, Atlantic and Pacific, from rushing rivers, and roaring floods, and whispering brooks, and the plash of thunder-showers, and the sweet ripple of the refreshing rain, and the noiseless falling of the gentle dew, and they would all go up together in such a voice as none could utter, and unless they were where God is, none would have ears to hear. God alone can fully and always hear the voice that the earth utters to the sky by the many tongues of its many waters. But he sends us men sometimes to whom he has given such ears in their soul that they can perceive some of the meaning of the world's great sea voice, and they are able to translate for us some of the music and magic of the sea-soul of the earth. These men are poets, or painters, or musicians, and they can hear more than most of us, far more than we hear at the coast, of the great sea's musical mystery, the strange trouble of the weird waters, and the moving ocean's mighty joy. . . .

Now, mankind is a great, great sea, and the souls of men and women are like the waves which cover the face of the great deep. They are always in motion, and they utter many a sound of joy and grief, of laughter and woe. They clash against each other and foam; they throw themselves against the hard shore of law and fate; and they hiss and rage. They join again hand in hand and dance to each other in life's sunshine, and laugh, and sport, and answer gaily to the blue sky. We can see, among the people we meet and know, how different they are from each other, and how differently they feel at different times, and how differently they express themselves. They are now quiet, now merry, now busy, now full of praise and joy; again, they are sad, restless, crying, sobbing may be, or even wailing and gnashing their teeth. The moods of the soul are more than the shades of the sea, and the heart's sounds are more manifold than the voices of the waters. Babies are crying and crowing, boys are shouting, while the girls whisper, and the birds sing; women are smiling and rippling with gladness and moving among men like a quiet tune; again they are full of fierce jealousies, hatreds, and bitter words, or they are crushed with grief for the little ones to whom they used to sing. Men are lustily moving about their noisy business, shouting in public conflict, preaching quiet or jubilant truth, or, again, cursing God and each other, or groaning beneath blows and losses from which they never rise. All these moods and sounds of the soul we see and hear, both within us and around us, and they make altogether a strange and mysterious tone. The voice of our own hearts is more than we can fathom—it is so manifold, so mingled, so confused. How unfathomable, then, is the one sound of all those souls whom day by day we meet and look out on, as we look at the waves from the shore! But if we could hear, not our own hearts only, nor the heart's utterance of our own little circle, but the sound

of the great human heart all the world over, and the
sound of all the hearts that ever have lived or shall
live, what a strange and awful voice that would be? If
we could go to some magic hole and put our ear where
we could hear the beatings, the chafings, the music of
the whole human soul and the whole world's heart,
what a great and dreadful sound that would be! If we
could only sit up there with God, where it all rises to,
and comes up like one mighty tune, so sad, so solemn,
so glorious, like an eternal organ; if we could only get
one of these messengers of God, like the poets and musicians who caught and sang the great music of the sea—
if we could get some such one to gather up for us all the
many little voices that rise from the restless sea of
sounding human souls and speak it out again for us,
with the voice of God thrown in, and the awfulness of
the music made divine, what a voice his would be,
sweet, full, mighty, mysterious, solemn! What a voice!
—rich like all instruments, piercing like a sword, never
to be forgotten, like the loveliest of all our dreams.

Now it is no dream but a truth. God has sent us such
a man. He has sent us a soul in whom there sounds the
echo of those many waters, which I have described as
the stir, and passion, and glow, and pain of the great
human soul. He has sent us Jesus Christ. There is no
movement of the human heart to which he does not
answer and sympathize. All that people rejoice in and
all that they suffer rests in the heart of Christ. He is like
the cleft in the rock where we can hear the whole
restless human heart below, sounding so awful and
strange. When we feel in sympathy with Jesus it is as if
we were taken up to God's right hand, and heard all
the still, sad music of mankind rising in a wondrous key
and complete tune. When we understand Jesus we get
such a deep, sweet knowledge of the human soul as we

get of the music of the sea from the poets and musicians. That is the meaning when it is said, 'His voice is as the sound of many waters.' All the thoughts, feelings, and actions of the human soul are like waves of the sea; and altogether they make a mysterious and solemn sound like the voice of the ocean; and the one voice which gathers up for us all these sounds by his deep sympathy, and lets us hear its sweet and manifold solemnity, is the voice of Jesus. And so it is because of his deep, true sympathy with little waves like you or me that he gives out the vast music of all such waves together, and his voice is as the sound of many waters— so huge, so soft, so musical, so mysterious, so grand, sometimes so terrible.

—Pulpit Parables for Young Hearers

The Room of Mirrors

If I wanted to drive anybody in my power into misery and madness, I think I know a way in which it could be done. I would suggest that they should be put into a room which was covered all over the walls and ceiling with mirrors; and I would let nobody see them, and I should never let them out; they would speak to nobody; they should be left in solitary confinement, only not in the dark. No, I would give them plenty of light—that would be part of my plan. And there would be no windows to look out at, the light should all come from above. And it should come through frosted glass panes, so that the blue sky could never be seen. But the only thing they should see would be themselves over and over and over again in these mirrors. And every time they moved a limb a hundred limbs would move around them, and every wink should be answered by a shower of winks, and every time they lifted their eyes hundreds of eyes would stare at them from all sides, and if they got up in a rage a hundred men would rage and dance to keep them company, and if they raised their faces to the sky there would be no sky, but scores of their own terrified faces looking down upon them day after day. They would have no companions round them, only images of themselves mocking every movement; and they would have no face of God over them, only reflections of their own face and their own passions. Can you conceive how horrible this would grow to be? Don't you think it would send anybody crazy before very long? I am sure it would. They might find a little amusement in it at first, but at last it would be dreadful and more than they could bear.

Now just as man would go mad if he had no society but his own image, so those people who move about in pure self-seeking go what we might call morally mad. They are sane and wise enough to transact business; they don't go off their heads, but they go off their hearts. It is a derangement, not of the wits, but of the conscience. And they become poor, miserable, detested beings, though they may grow as rich as you like to think. They lose all the wisdom of the heart and all the wealth of love. They dwindle and dwindle, if you could see their soul, like a prowling spider or a starving cat. They wither and shrivel into nothing, because they go about seeking to be everything. Amid their wealth and power their soul goes flickering and spluttering out, like a candle-end in a gold chandelier.

—*Pulpit Parables for Young Hearers*

I WAS living a few weeks ago up among my own Scottish hills. And day by day the sun shone on them, and night by night they were looked on by the harvest moon. Day by day I gazed at their lovely faces, and night by night I thought how beautifully they slept. From top to bottom they were dressed in purple, and the morning mist clothed them like fine linen. Solomon in all his glory was not arrayed like one of these. August is the month for the heather bloom, and heather clothed these hills as with a garment seamless from head to foot. Every day that picture was hung up before me, and every hour almost the changing light of the sky made a new shade pass upon that purple robe. Now it was dark, deep, almost blue. Again it was bright, clear, almost pink. It changed from glory to glory. And every evening the sunset made storms of solemn glory among the tumultuous clouds, and heaven showed lovelier than the lovely hills. The colours of earth are nothing to the colours of the glowing sky. Fiery red, and tawny gold, and sweet pale green were there. Fiery red in the waves and billows that the long clouds made; tawny gold on the yellow sand where they seemed to gently break; sweet pale green in the peaceful pools that slumbered deep in cloudland's pathless and eternal rest. And pearl and pink, orange and blue, violet and purple were up there, mingled in a sweet unrest and calm commotion. And the sky above and the hills below, made as it were a picture of some high holy land, and it was good to be there.

All this rose before my mind as I passed a shop window in an ugly London street the other day. What did I see? Nothing but a few sprays of flowery heather, a few scraggy and faded twigs of that hardy purple which had clothed whole hills beneath gorgeous skies. That was all, but it was enough. These poor little branches opened heaven to me as it were, and all the sights I had been used to see came back with a rush.

Now that is how the sight of children, no matter how ragged, poor, or tiny, made Jesus think of the sweet glories of heaven where crowds of children do constantly behold the face of the Father.

—Pulpit Parables for Young Hearers

Anthology Part VIII

PASTORALIA
SPIRITUAL DIRECTIONS GIVEN TO HIS STUDENTS

The cure of souls must begin at home.

P.T.F.

Salvation our First Concern

BEWARE lest Christ become more for your imagination, or for your admiration, than for your salvation.

—Address

Concentrating on Christ

WE must allow a great many books to go unread, and a great many social visits unpaid, in order that we may concentrate on Christ.

—Address, Luke 10, 41-42

On Getting in Front of Christ

IT is possible to be so active in the service of Christ as to forget to love him. Many a man preaches Christ but gets in front of him by the multiplicity of his own works. It will be your ruin if you do! Christ can do without your works, what he wants is you. Yet if he really has you he will have all your works.

—Address, Matthew 7, 21

Christ our Minister

CHRIST came not to be ministered to, but to minister; and our first duty, therefore, is to be ministered to by him. First faith, then works.

—Address, Luke 10, 41-42

Faith in Christ, Not in Faith

THE cultivation of the soul is best carried out by the cultivation of faith. But our faith should not be faith in faith, but faith in Christ. The height of faith is to lose sight of itself in Christ. Trying to be good is a subtle temptation to many of us, but true goodness is unconscious of itself. It is like humility, which Luther calls 'the eye that sees every thing but itself.' Such goodness is the natural product of faith in Christ.

—Address, 1 Timothy 4, 7

We 'Find Ourselves' in the Arena of Life

AS a rule God is not found by waiting in the wilderness alone. He found Elijah there, but he sent him back into the world of men. We find ourselves amongst men, not by sitting down, folding our hands, and waiting for miracles.

—Address, Psalm 55, 6

Rest is good so long as we recognize that the true end of

life is not resting but victory. The rest of God is the power of God, the truest rest of all is an accession of strength. The motto of the world is 'Onward!' The motto of the saint is 'Upward!' but the motto of the Cross is 'Inward!' You have acquired a real spiritual culture when you realize that you can only find the onward and the upward through the inward.

—Address, Psalm 55, 6

The Cure of Souls must begin at Home

Exercise thyself rather unto godliness—1 Timothy 4, 7

Christianity is much harder than any asceticism. How hard it is to be a Christian. It is freedom, but true freedom is only possible under discipline, and the greater the aim the more discipline is required. The simplicity of Greek sculpture is due to its utmost severity.

To have a real religious experience is a hard thing, and demands the severest discipline. Religion is cursed by hundreds of people who have never known it.

O could I tell, ye surely would believe it!
O could I only say what I have seen!
How should I tell or how should ye receive it,
How till he bringeth you where I have been?

It means the greatest exertion to be godly, and still more to grow in godliness. The discipline we undertake is not to get rid of sin, but for godliness. We seek not to be saved but to be right. You have to exercise your own soul before you exercise the souls of others. The cure of souls must begin at home.

Again you are to exercise yourself for the sake of godliness, not for your own sake. Mere self-culture is

worth very little. For this reason the best type of godliness is possible only in a society, that is in the Church,
or the Household of Faith.

—Address, 1 Timothy 4, 7

The Freedom the Bible Creates

WE all need the freedom the Bible creates for us. Our
great danger is not the slavery spoken against on social
and political platforms, but the slavery of complex
daily life. If you work for human relations and circles
you become a slave to them, if you work for Christ you
are free to adventure in all directions. You must learn
to descend upon your duties as Moses did from the
mountain.

—Address, Psalm 146, 3

Above All no Heroics

WE reach heaven step by step, fighting all the way.
What we need most of all for this life is the courage of
the prosaic. As someone has put it, *above all no heroics*. If
we get into the habit of indulging in heroics we too
often end in a scream. Beware of the perorating spirit,
the life that is all rhetoric. Heroism is a great thing, but
fortitude is greater still.

You will have noted that the Psalmist speaks of the
wings of a dove; that suggests a horizontal flight. It
typifies longing for solitude. The prophet speaks of the
eagle's wings, suggesting flight upward in the face of the
sun. We very often crave for opiates when we should

seek tonics, and yet the truest warrior is he whose heart often turns to peace.

—*Address, Jeremiah 9, 2*

We are Christ's Curates

LEST you be overwhelmed with the greatness of your task, remember no church is given to any man without the Saviour of the Church and of him. After all it is Christ's Church more than yours. He is the real Pastor of every real Church, and the Bishop of its minister. You are but his curate.

—*Ordination Address*

The Nature of Faith

FAITH rolls the soul over on to God, and with the soul the world with its wonderful crooked aching past, its selfish unregenerate present, and its uncertain future. Faith realizes that the very judgements of God show that he will never let us go. If God loves us enough to punish us, all may yet be well. How could it be otherwise with a Creator? How we cleave to the work of our hands, the things on which we have spent our thought and time! No wonder God loves the world, since he has watched it grow through many ages, not just the soul but a world of souls. God and the world have lived long together.

Or think again of God's interest in making Jesus. He watched him grow from boyhood to childhood, and from childhood to glorious manhood. Like a human father, but much more closely and with much greater

112

understanding, He watched him as he went about doing good. He was with him through all the pain and shame of the Cross, and afterwards in the Resurrection triumph. Is it any wonder that he called him, 'My beloved Son'?

And then what about our re-making? God's greatest name is not Creator, but Re-creator, Redeemer. It is a tremendous thing to be able to say that the wreck and ruin of the world was as much within his power as the making of it at first from chaos. God is faithful to the souls he made, and always will be. He is faithful to the souls he made and died for, as he remakes them by suffering, first his own suffering and then theirs. Our very pain is a sign of God's remembrance of us, for it would be much worse if we were left in ghastly isolation. Be thankful that God cares enough for you to be angry with you.

—Address, 1 Peter 4, 19

Reconciliation better than Denunciation

OUR Christian work is social reconciliation rather than denunciation. We ministers especially are set free in the flesh that we may be bound in the spirit. We are bound to wrestle for the present mind of the Holy Spirit of our Redemption, and to acquire that deepest knowledge of the moral world which comes in no other way. It is by the anointing of the Holy that we know all things. And what does that mean? It means that thus alone we know things on the universal scale, in their historic and their eternal setting. It is thus that we take the deepest and broadest measure of human affairs, and apply to them in the most relevant way the standard of the Eternal.

To know men is one thing, to know man is another; and it is on man, not men, that Society turns. The men of holiness have often been, and oftener been called, ignorant of the world's ways. Ignorant of its conventions no doubt often, but not ignorant of its true structure, of its most imperturbable laws, of its first conditions, and of its final destiny. Moreover, many of them have been mighty men in the world's ways and wars, and have intervened to decisive Christian purpose in its affairs.

—A Holy Church the Moral Guide of Society

Puritanism may suffer from Purists

THERE is always room for heroism and need for martyrs; but Puritanism may suffer from purists. Moral purity is not a white soul *in vacuo*. It means doing our best spiritual duty by the situation in which we are placed, and making it easier for those who come after us to do better. And it ought to resent martyrdom dictated and organized from without.

—A Holy Church the Moral Guide of Society

Tragedy and Redemption

ONE reads somnambulant sermons about coming into tune with the infinite, about cultivating the presence of God, about pausing in life to hear the melodies of the everlasting chime, and all the rest of the romance of piety breathed beneath the moon in the green and pleasant glades of devotion—all without a hint of the classic redemption, or even of the Christ, whereby alone we have access to any of the rich quietives of faith. The preacher has glimpses of the paradise, but no sense of the purgatorio. He has the language but not the accent of that far heavenly country. O! but we want men who have been there and been naturalized there. We want more than romantic and temperamental piety. We want the accent of the Holy Ghost, learned with a new life at its classic capital—the Cross. We want something more than a lovely Gospel with the fine austerity of a cloistered ethic. I do not wonder that the literary people react from self-conscious Galahad, sure and vain of his own purity, and turn to welcome the smell of the good brown earth. So also our virile sinfulness turns from the criticisms of fastidious religion to the *blood* of Christ and the cost at which we are scarcely saved. It was not Galahad or Arthur that drew Christ from heaven. It was a Lancelot race. It was a tragic issue of man's passion that called out the glory of Christ. It is a most tragic world, this, for those who see to the bottom of it and leave us their witness to its confusion, as Shakespeare did in *Hamlet*, *Lear*, and even *The Tempest*. He had to leave it there, stated in pathetic majesty but unreconciled. But what that mighty age could not do in Shakespeare it did in its Puritans. They had found a reconcilement which belonged to a larger world than Shakespeare's, and a deeper vision than that of solemn tragedy. For their life was no tragedy, but a redemption going beneath the foundations of the world. It was a redemption that had gone through tragedy and come out at the other side, in a solemn music and divine comedy. They were more than Shakespearian; they were Dantesque. They had realized more than the fate of sin; they had measured its guilt. They knew what it cost man in happiness; but they knew still more what it cost God in the Cross. They knew the tragedy of life which makes man man; but still more they knew the redemption which makes God God.

—The Grace of the Gospel as the Moral Authority in the Church

The Sanctity of Economics

To hear some talk you would think that making money was a crime, and the whole end of business making money. It is not so. Trade with its profits is absolutely needful for the employment and comfort of mankind, and for eliciting the resources of both men and Nature. It is a contribution, or we may make it so, to the spirit of that same love which sustains, saves, and develops mankind.

—A Holy Church the Moral Guide of Society

Renew the Youth of your Soul

How can a man be born when he is old?
John 3, 4

NICODEMUS was a pillar of his church, yet he came to a young Rabbi, which suggests that his faith must have been seriously shaken, and he himself profoundly disturbed. The truth is he had more passion for life than power to live. There are many people like that, some through physical weakness, and some from more deep rooted cause. But whatever the cause it is a painful experience.

The meaning of this question is, How can I recover my soul's life and youth? It was full life, not long life, he wanted, but how can a man go back upon himself and begin again? Can we ever grow young again in soul? When ideals are disillusioned does it mean that there are no greater ideals beyond? *They that wait upon the Lord shall renew their strength,* is that mere poetry?

New knowledge may fail to rejuvenate, but there remains a new experience—*regeneration.* Religious interest may be strong, moral puritanism intense, zeal for the Kingdom eager without an experience of rebirth, regeneration. There are many religious people, both teachers and taught, who have never experienced eternal life through the new birth.

Eternal life is a far more searching thing than the Kingdom of God. We may live for the Kingdom and yet never have eternal life. John the Baptist was great, but not so great as the least in the Kingdom of those who are born again.

We can never erase the line between the Church and the World, between the spirit and the flesh, between those who are born and those who are born again.

It is one thing to be influenced by the principles of the Kingdom, and quite another to be in the Kingdom.

—Manuscript Addresses to Students

There came a woman having an alabaster box of ointment
Mark 14, 3

THIS chapter begins the history of the Passion, and this
story is like a star on the edge of the Passion cloud.

Firstly: the woman is not named. The work stands and
the worker goes, at least as far as man is concerned. She
belongs to the true aristocracy whose deeds outlive their
names.

Secondly: mark the dumb eloquence of this woman.
The eloquence of action is the greatest thing in the
world.

Thirdly: what a delight this service was to Jesus. It was
a fine devotion, finely and fitly expressed. It was a
beautiful incident but it was more beautifully received.
He turned to defend her from her critics. It was this
which made Thomas Dekker describe him as *the
first true gentleman that ever breathed*. Look at the mag-
nificent interpretation he put upon the act. It was
far greater than she thought. She meant it finely, but it
was taken more finely still. That is how God always
takes our acts of worship.

Fourthly: notice how sure Jesus was of his own power.
He knew that he could make her immortal. He was to
make her immortal in history, but he had already
ensured her immortality in Heaven. *Notwithstanding
in this rejoice not . . . but rather rejoice, because your names are
written in heaven.*

Fifthly: what is rewarded is not her loving nature but her
love for Christ. The Gospel demands not love but faith,
and piety only as it is created by faith. It is much more to

118

love Christ than to love man; we love men most when we love them for Christ's sake.

Judas sold his Master for £3 10. 0.; that was his estimate of his Master. Hers was this ointment which cost £10, and she would have given more had she possessed it. Pedantry and economy need sometimes to be taught a lesson. There was a mathematician once who complained of *Paradise Lost* that it proved nothing! There are many who complain of Christian worship today on the same ground. The greatest work that any soul can do is to worship. We need to learn the utility of the useless. Even to think of the poor may sometimes be wrong, if it hinders us from remembering God and his Christ. The saying 'Work *is* worship' is not wholly true. It is untrue unless we also remember that worship is work.

—Manuscript Addresses to Students

Be People of Power, not of Problems

Not as though I had already attained . . .
Philippians 3, 12

ONE of our problems is that while we have a perfect Word we ourselves are imperfect. How can the Word and the man be made to coincide? In spirit if not in compass we may coincide, that is we may move upon the same centre. Note two things about Paul in this connection. First his modesty, and then his confidence. *His modesty.* He is more satisfied with his goal than with his attainment. His modesty is not due to diffidence, but to the great conception he had of his Gospel. It was not due to the great problem he faced, but to the greatness of the power given him to deal with it.

The minister of the Gospel is not a man of problems first of all, but a man of power. He should know the greatness of the world within more thoroughly than the greatness of the problems about him: *because greater is he that is in you, than he that is in the world.*

Paul was much more sure of the Gospel's grasp of him than of his grasp of the Gospel. In your ministry you must trust not in what you bring with you from your books, but him whom you bring with you to your books, and to everything else in life.

His confidence. There was nothing Paul was so sure of as the grace of Christ. He was not so much concerned about his own experience as about him who brought that experience. His own experience was used by him to irradiate Christ.

Paul was the apostle of a Gospel which had broken him up, and would have ruined him, if it had not saved him.

To be able to say at any stage in life 'I have everything that God can give,' is to have the victory that overcomes the world. But distinguish this from saying, 'I have everything that heart can wish'. There are things you cannot have now because you are not ready for them, and because of the exigencies of the Kingdom of God.

—Manuscript Addresses to Students

As his majesty is, so is his mercy
Ecclesiasticus 2, 18

WHAT is the true nature of the divine majesty? It is not material vastness, nor the majesty of force, nor the majesty of mystery. It is not the majesty of thought, great as thought is. The true majesty of God is his mercy. That is the thing he did which a man would never have done—he had mercy on all flesh.

His greatness was not in his loftiness, but in his nearness. He was great not because he was above feelings, but because he could feel as no man could. God's majesty is saturated through and through with his forgiving love, which comes out most of all in his treatment of sin. Do we feel enough the moral majesty of the Cross? Have we ever really felt the majesty of God's mercy?

What then in the second place is the nature of the divine mercy? God's mercy is not weak, for it belongs to the nature of his moral majesty. God does not save with a fragment of himself. The whole God is in you and for you.

We pity misfortune with part of ourselves, but God pities us with his all. God saves to the uttermost, but it is with his uttermost, all he has. It took all his moral energy to save us. All the love and power in the universe are at work saving us. We are not saved by a mere turn of God's hand, but by the whole mighty power of the Cross. With us mercy belongs to our spare time, with God mercy is his business. Beneath us are the everlasting arms, and they are there to embrace, lift, hold and save us; not rocks, mark you, nor strong foundations, but arms. The mercy of God is so near and so great that often we cannot see it. The Cross is a strange symbol of mercy. The pathos of life, and its terrible suffering, the ignorance of many, the dangers to which both young and old are exposed, the shattered hopes, and over all this nature's harsh cruel laws; all these things appal you? But turn and see the overwhelming mercy of God. *As his majesty is, so is his mercy.* We know something of the compassions of men, and feel them ourselves. What then must the compassions of God be? What if they showed themselves in the Cross, with its extremity of suffering, its appalling shame, its utter abandonment of love.

If the Cross is not God's mercy, then it is his arraignment before the world.

—Manuscript Addresses to Students

Realize the Living God

The church of the living God
1 Timothy 3, 15

NOTE particularly the phrase *the living God.* The living God is the basis of the living Church. We must try to get home to people the idea of the Divine Personality. You know what an over-mastering personality is, a magnetic man. He gives you a sense of power which dominates you. Such a power is Christ and the living God.

We do not want people with views and sympathies, but men of conviction, men, that is, with an experience of God that grows with the years. We must feel the grip of Christ, which we felt in the mighty business which made us Christians, and feel it for ever; so that when we lose our power to hold Christ he shall stand over and hold us. Conversion may change its form, but it must never lose its power.

We need the living God, for we need something as great as God over us, and we need something as mighty as human life is. How can we face the corporate life which is before us today? Only in the experience of a God who is mightier than life.

Then we need a God as near to us as life is. We must have a searching and a shaping God. This we have in the Son of the Living God. The end of all our piety is to realize the living God. Here we find how much more than historic was Christ, especially in his Cross.

The Living God alone can make us living men; the mighty God alone can make us mighty men; the loving God alone can make us consecrated men.

—Manuscript Addresses to Students

Let God Guide

I will guide thee with mine eye
Psalm 32, 8

THIS means that we are guided by intelligent sympathy. There are as many people who cannot see God as there are who refuse to follow him. We are often at a loss to know what the will of God really is, but if God knows and feels for all souls, then he acts for and in all things, and all souls; and that is his providence.

In our exalted moments, and in luminous personalities we recognize God, but in the periods of darkness in our experience and in the world's history,

God is working unseen. Even then, however, if we have a due sense of responsibility we are being guided by him. Paul was guided by the Spirit when he made judgements on the data before him. Or again if you pray you are being guided by God. The very act of prayer, apart from the answer, is the guidance of God. The action of God upon us in prayer is just as real as our action upon him. The guidance of the godly is the guidance of God, but how are we to discern it? That is an art, and it comes late in life and not early. It needs much cultivation. To believe in God's guidance is one thing, to understand it is a very different thing. A man may be a mystic and yet not a saint; a saint is a man who can read the will of God, and whose judgement is therefore reliable. The great High School for this discernment is prayer. In prayer we must battle for discernment as we battle for our faith. Finally the source of all our belief in Providence is the Cross, in which God is always acting upon us for his Kingdom.

—Manuscript Addresses to Students

Fight the Good Fight of Faith

I have fought a good fight
2 Timothy 4, 7

THIS is a great retrospect. *I have finished my course.* Life is made up of ends and of beginnings. Death is but the greatest crisis of many, and all crises are like Janus in the Roman Pantheon, two-faced. The end of one crisis is the beginning of another. But with all the ebbs and flows of life there must be a unity, some grand unity which constitutes life's reality. For us that unity is, in

Paul's phrase, '*For me to live is Christ,*' that is, Christ is my career.

The unity of our life is therefore objective, outside ourselves. It is not in the evolution of life but in its goal. When Wordsworth writes of a life whose days are bound each to each by natural piety, he is not truly Christian. When a man is truly Christian each day is bound to Christ, is devoted to him, is lived in him. Life is not realizing a plan, but fulfilling a mission. Thus a broken column in a churchyard, symbolizing a broken life, is an anachronism. There is no such thing as a broken life for the man of faith. All life is complete in Christ, and always complete, no matter when the end come, the course is finished.

The keeping of our souls is in the hand of Christ. Paul did not keep his soul, he kept the faith. No apostle starts out with Paracelsus' ambition, *I go to prove my soul.* That grand confidence is so often broken as it was with Paracelsus. An apostle has a charge, a trust. Paracelsus has an instinct he is going to follow with God's help, but the Christian is not working out anything that is within, instead he is laying hold of eternal life.

Yet there is a warfare to wage and something to prove. Paul's greatest triumph was, not that he had worked out any instinct, still less that he had done any great works, but that he had kept the faith. The Christian man is fighting bigger battles than anything he has to face in business. It is a great warfare. All uncouth passions must be mastered, everything so natural to ordinary men must be carefully sifted and judged upon. He will know what it is to be forced down upon his knees again and again in the battle, even forced into the dust. It is a hard thing to be faithful in this calling but it is a terrible thing to fail. You have to cope, not only with ordinary things, but you have to fight for your Gospel, for your faith. You have to war your way onward to a deeper grasp of that Gospel with which you began. It is a great thing when a man, after facing the doubts and scepticism of the age, as well as those that are brought to him in his College course, is able to say, *I am trusting the same grace now that I did at the beginning.*

The great thing is to keep our faith. Not being so full of love to Christ as to have confidence, but being so full of confidence in God's changeless, profound, and most wonderful love in Jesus Christ. It is not the love that *I once felt* that saves us, but Christ's most wonderful love for us in the Cross. O, what a fight it is, this fight for such a faith in such a Christ!

—*Manuscript Addresses to Students*

Beware of Fits of Confession

I could not see for the glory of that light

Acts 22, 11

THERE is a blindness that is due to want of light. We need not dwell on that. There is also a blindness which comes from excess of light. The egoism of youth is such a blindness. The true vision only comes when the Light of life comes to us. When Christ becomes our source of vision, and our power of seeing, we get the right vision. It is part of his schooling in life to enable us to take the true measure of all things, of God first of all and then of ourselves. Christ places us at the centre of all things, the true view point.

Chalmers spoke of *the expulsive power of a new affection*. When Christ comes in he turns out the worst part of a man's nature. By his light he hides certain things from us. You will not see the meaner side of life, or if you see it you will rise above it, and live among the great, mighty, positive realities of God and the soul. Christ says, *Be of good cheer; I have overcome the world*, and it is in that world where he has overcome we are called upon to live. Then you will not dwell too much on the faults of others, for you will be far too much taken up with the glorious perfection of Christ.

Again, Christ hides from us ourselves and our own subjectivity. There is a kind of piety which thinks more of self and its short-comings than of Christ and his victory. Beware of fits of confession, they are generally morbid. Confession should generally be made only to God, and even then thanksgiving is the first thing, confession is secondary. The most blessed thing of all is that in Christ our sins are hidden.

Beware of the small noisy lights, lest you miss the great Light. As Emerson has told us, *when half-gods go, the gods arrive*. Humanity often obscures Christ, but never forget that he is the great light, and only in him do we get the right vision.

—*Manuscript Addresses to Students*

Think More of the Depth of God than the Depth of Your Cry

Out of the depths have I cried unto thee, O Lord
                                        Psalm 130, 1

THIS is a cry of humility rather than despair. It is from a man who has been in the depths. Some have never been in the depths and have never been drawn to the heights. Real gratitude, humility and confidence, which lifts a man to the heights, is that which has been drawn from the depths.

This cry is alien to our age. Sometimes the Church is free from the sense of sin, but ever and again the sense of it sweeps over the world as it did at the Reformation.

It is strange, too, to a self-reliant race like ours. Yet in our age and our race there is a great sadness abroad, *the pessimism of the age.*

How very human the cry is. As yet there have been more depths than heights in history. With all our successes and progress there is mostly labour and sorrow. Most people spend the greater part of their days on the grey level if not in the depths. It is dreadful to find how many people live quite alone, no friends, no helps along the way. Even today man is felt to be man by his superior capacity to suffer.

But the depth is simply the height inverted, as sin is the index of moral grandeur. The cry is not only truly human, but divine as well. God is deeper than the deepest depth in man. He is holier than our deepest sin is deep. There is no depth so deep to us as when God reveals his holiness in dealing with our sin, *Greater is he that is in you, than he that is in the world.*

The New Testament does not think about limitation but about power. It deals in ethical, not in philosophical categories. The deepest depth of God's love is deeper than the deepest depth of man's hate. Man cannot hate infinitely, but God can love infinitely.

The depth to which you cry is outside yourself. Think more of the depth of God than the depth of your cry. The worst thing that can happen to a man is to have no God to cry to out of the depth. The deepest depth of all outside of God is separation from God. You can often do more with wild sinners than with indifferent weaklings.

First then we cry from the depth of our need, then from the depth of our sin and despair, and finally deepest of all we cry from the depth of our faith, which lifts us to the heights. We know then that if we fall, we fall deeper into the arms of God, *If my bark sink, 'tis but to another sea*. For as our hell is deep, so is our heaven deep; our hell is so deep because we were made for so deep a heaven.

—Manuscript Addresses to Students

Remember it is Christ's Church more than Yours

ORDINATION ADDRESS

October 20th, 1909

I have manifested thy name unto the men which thou gavest me out of the world: thine they were, and thou gavest them me.
John 17, 6

THREE things are suggested by this text: the *Property*, the *Gift*, the *Use*.

1. *Thine they were*. These people are God's people, Christ's people, not yours. You say they are my people. Yes, but only because they are the People of God.

To begin with, they cost him more than they will ever cost you. If ever they are trying, and if ever they tax your patience, remember that. And if ever you feel unequal to your task remember that they are more his than yours, because they cost him more. Your church is not in chief a Congregational church, still less is it your church; it is the Church of the living God, bought by Christ's most precious blood.

You will see then that the Church is composed of those who are his people in a very different sense than, for instance, *the earth is the Lord's*. The Spirit of the Lord fills and moves his creation, but what made the Church, and fills and moves it is his Holy Spirit, something dearer, something greater. All men are God's, as part of his creation, they are his offspring, but there is something greater, diviner than humanity; it is the Church of God. The Church of God is the finest product of humanity, it is the greatest thing in the universe. And this is so because it was produced by God in his Son and Holy Spirit. The Church is his own as no nation is, no society, no family. The Church is his as his Son is his, his in his Son. His not as a part of creation, but as a new creation in Jesus Christ. If in love he created the world, in much more love did he create the Church. It was in might and beauty he created the world; it was in holy love he created the Church. It is his as nothing else in the world is. It is the Church of his Son, and his Son is more to him than all the world.

I speak of the Church of course as God sees it, God who sees the end from the beginning. You must also learn to see your Church like that, not as a man sees it but as God redeemed it, and as God trusts it, and bears with it, and feeds it, and serves it, and waits for it while it grows to the mature man in Jesus Christ.

2. I have spoken of the property, I now come to speak of the *gift*. *Thou gavest them to me.* Your ordination is an act and gift of God. He is putting his people into your hands. He does not so much give you a position as a trust. He puts this church in your care. But it is also true that he entrusts this church with you. If they treat you ill it will affect your whole life, and just the same if they treat you well. A minister is very much what his first church makes him. But let them remember this,

that to treat you well they must treat your Gospel better than you.

Therefore it is not popularity you must think about first. Do not crave morbidly for your people's love. Craving does not bring it, and often arrests it. Do not beg for sympathy. Think of your church from the other point of view, as a trust from God to whom you must be faithful in it. This flock is committed to you by God. You do not simply take each other, but as in a true marriage God has given you to each other. This is really a marriage ceremony. You are being married to the church. This will comfort you when you are doubting if you should be at this work. Say to yourself, *Thou hast given them to me, the responsibility is thine. Da quod jubes, et jubes quod vis. I am not worthy. Yes, that is true, but what is that to thee, follow thou me.*

Of course you are not worthy to preach the Gospel, none of us is worthy. But then your people are not worthy to hear it. If it depended on worth there would be neither preacher nor listeners. The worth is where the power is, in Christ and God, who does not give us according to our deserts.

Lest you be overwhelmed with the greatness of your task, remember no church is given to any man without the Saviour of the Church and of him. After all it is Christ's Church more than yours. He is the real Pastor of every real church, and the Bishop of its minister. You are but his curate.

3. Finally, the *use* of the gift. *I have manifested thy name unto them.* What a charge—to be the living man on whom men depend for the living God! The people say to you as minister, what Philip said to Jesus, *Shew us the Father. I have manifested thy name.* That means *nature*, and nature means presence and action—not truth about God, but God himself in action. It is not

the Fatherhood of God you have to preach, but God the Father. You have not to preach about God to people, you must preach God into people. So true preaching is not telling people, but acting on people, making people. No amount of telling will ever convince people of the Father, it has to be lived into them. Therefore yours must be a personal ministry. When the personal God revealed himself it was in the person of his Son Jesus Christ, and when Christ is to be preached it is by man, by a soul. You cannot reveal the Holy One by talking about holiness. *That is true*, says someone. *You can only reveal the Holy One by being holy*. But he knows little of himself who can say that. If we cannot preach the Holy God except by being holy, who can preach him? The holiness that fits you to preach about the holy is not your personal sanctity and conduct, but your evident communion with the Holy Christ. It is a life of faith you want more than a life of conduct.

Why! Paul addressed such churches as his by the name *Saints!* Churches in which the grossest sins were evident. They were not saints by conduct but by faith. Your goodness is not equal to your task as a minister but your faith must be. You must realize that *My grace is sufficient for thee*. So it is! Not even your faith is sufficient, but only his grace; for you have to reveal Christ as Christ revealed, in this sense, that in both cases it is the soul that tells. But there is this difference. He revealed God to us by the resources of his own soul, while you cannot do it from the resources of your soul but only from his. Nobody was for him what he is for you with God.

The greatest thing you can give any man is your God and your Saviour. The reason why some ministers are valuable for other things than preaching, even valuable in spite of their preaching, is that they preach about

God, and about Christ, they do not preach Christ. They are only messengers, not sacraments.

A favourite type of preaching today is to analyse your soul; it is subjective, psychological preaching. It is weak, it is exhausting, it is dangerous. Analyse the Gospel in reference to the soul. You are a minister of the Word, not of the soul. And that word will be selective. There is real truth in the doctrine of Election. You will not appeal to all alike. To try to do so is to make your Gospel colourless. There will be some whom you will not touch. On the other hand there may be some given to you whom others have never touched.

If your church were smaller it might be more powerful. If you could shed off people as Christ did, you might be stronger like Gideon's host. Christ alone has the promise and reversion of all men, and he only at the last. At first all forsook him and fled

You have but a corner of the vineyard, and cannot appeal to all men; humility then is a better equipment than ambition, even the ambition of doing much good. And remember as a last word, in the Christian ministry all self-seeking is fatal.

—Manuscript Addresses to Students

Valedictory

Stewards of the mysteries of God
Corinthians 4, 1

I AM about to speak to those, or more especially to those, who are gathered here for the last time at an evening service. You are about to go into the active ministry, and to become stewards of the mysteries

133

of God, and I would have you realize how great is the work to which you have been called, and what will be expected of you by God.

The text divides itself into three parts: Stewards, Mysteries, and God.

1. You are first of all *stewards*, not owners. Men with a trust, not men with a property. You have to carry what many others have tried to carry, a Gospel, a Truth many times uttered. And so I would warn you not to strive to win notice by originality but only by the Gospel you preach. The truest things you will have to say are those that have been said many times, but they are still the most original. Grace is the most original thing in the world. However original sin may be, Grace is more original still. The Grace of God is so original as to be unexplainable.

It is a great thing to have gifts to bring home to your hearers, truths, great truths, in a clever way, but remember always that the essential thing for a minister is not gifts but faithfulness. Faithfulness not to your people but to God.

Where most ministers fail is in forgetting themselves. You yourself are part of God's trust to you. Not only to subdue your passions, and purify your life, but also to look after the method of your work. Plan out every day as though you worked for an earthly master, and had to give an account of your time. Your time is not your own, and every moment of it must be used to some purpose. Your time is not your own, it is God's.

But a minister's life is terribly difficult, and this is where the difficulty lies—every preacher has to be the greatest dogmatist and the humblest man in his church. I have often told you that a man had better not be a preacher at all if he is not a dogmatist. It is not preaching to give utterance to a great sympathy, but to

134

dogmatize about a definite Gospel. Nevertheless the minister must be the humblest man in his church. He must realize the great responsibility and privilege of his position, and his own inadequacy.

So perhaps the art of living as a minister is far more difficult than the art of preaching, and there is only one power that can help you, and that is communion with Christ. No amount of service to men can ever compensate you for neglecting communion with Christ. The minister must know by personal contact the living Christ, and all his ministry will be spoiled unless he does.

And this leads me to my second point.

2. You are stewards in charge of a *mystery*. Now a mystery does not mean a Sacrament, it does not even mean something mysterious. The mysteries of God are to be preached upon the housetops. Mystery here means type, symbol, parable. When Paul says, 'I will show you a mystery,' he means 'I will make clear to you by parable.' The mysteries of God mean knowledge, not due to man's discovery, but to God's revealing grace.

The great mystery of God is found in the Gospel, and a great and wonderful mystery it is. In all our search into it we must never cease to be awed and impressed by it. Never make light of your vocation as a revealer of the mysteries of God. That never can be reverenced on Sunday which is made light of during the week.

But your duty as preachers is not to preach sermons, but to preach a Gospel. What you have to dispense to the people is not anything of yours but a revelation of God's, a mystery The great storehouse of this mystery is the Bible. The Bible is your source. If you learn from other people you will begin at once to imitate them, and you will imitate their bad points, for their good ones belong to their own personality, and were obtained through the Bible only. If you would be as the great men of the Church you must obtain your personality where they obtained theirs. Christ alone can draw out the secret of your personality.

3. Now lastly. These mysteries are *God's*. We are in trust of the last and holiest reality of the world, the grace of God. Next to grace the deepest thing in the world is sin. That which went deeper than sin and overcame it, is that of which we are in charge.

It is an insoluble mystery of an insoluble God. If we could solve God we could solve the world, but at the same time he would cease to be God. God is insoluble, yet nevertheless he has solved himself by revelation. The great problem of life is solved by God himself. Shakespeare puts the question supremely, God answers it finally. See how great is the Gospel of which you are in charge. Rise to the dignity, the true dignity of the Cross! *Noblesse oblige!* It will save you, let it save you! Beware of your conduct. Be genial, be sociable. O yes, but never lose sight of your high calling, never lose sight of Christ, God's greatest mystery, your greatest power.

May he bless you and keep you. May he make his face to shine upon you, and be gracious unto you. May he lift up the light of his countenance upon you and give you peace.

—*Manuscript Addresses to Students*

Index of Persons